St. John Travel Guide 2025

Busy Neighbors With Map & Images, St. Thomas, St. Croix, Virgin Islands National Park, Trails for Hiking, The Trunk Bay, Events And Festivals

CAROLE J. HARVEY

Copyright © 2024, Carole J. Harvey. All rights reserved.

No part of this publication may be reproduced, distributed, or transmitted in any form or by any means, including photocopying, recording, or other electronic or mechanical methods, without the prior written permission of the publisher, except in the case of brief quotations embodied in critical reviews and certain other noncommercial uses permitted by copyright law.

Disclaimer

The information provided in this book is for general informational purposes only. While every effort has been made to ensure the accuracy and completeness of the information contained herein, the author and publisher assume no responsibility for any errors, omissions, or changes to travel details, prices, or locations. Readers are encouraged to verify any information with local authorities or service providers before making travel decisions. The author and publisher disclaim any liability for any personal, financial, or travel-related losses or damages incurred through the use of this guide.

Trademark

All product names, logos, and brands mentioned in this book are property of their respective trademark owners. Any use of trademarks or brand names is for descriptive purposes only and does not imply sponsorship, endorsement, or affiliation by or with the trademark holder

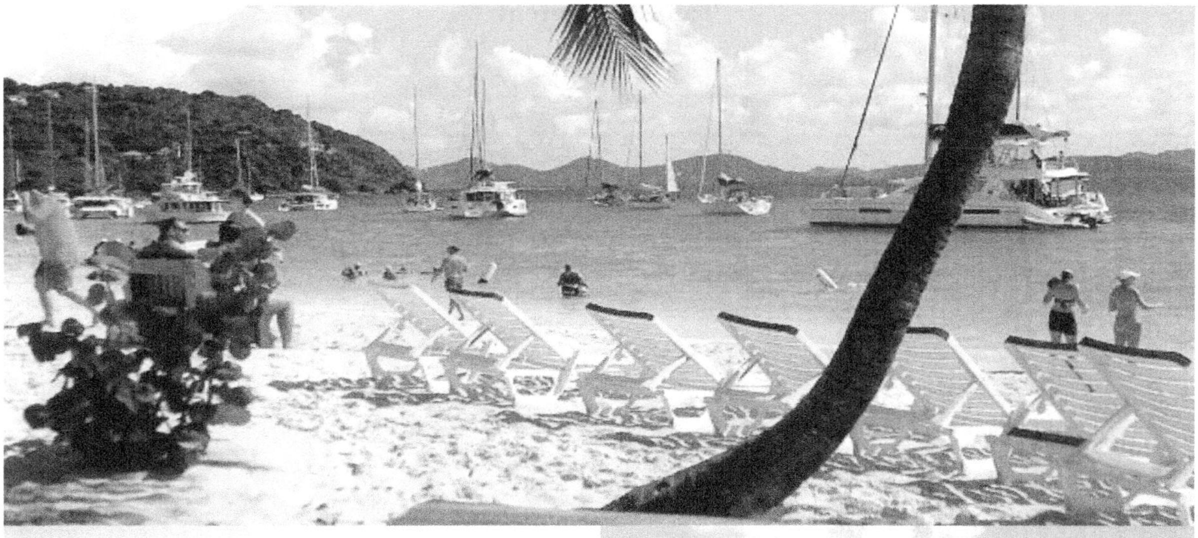
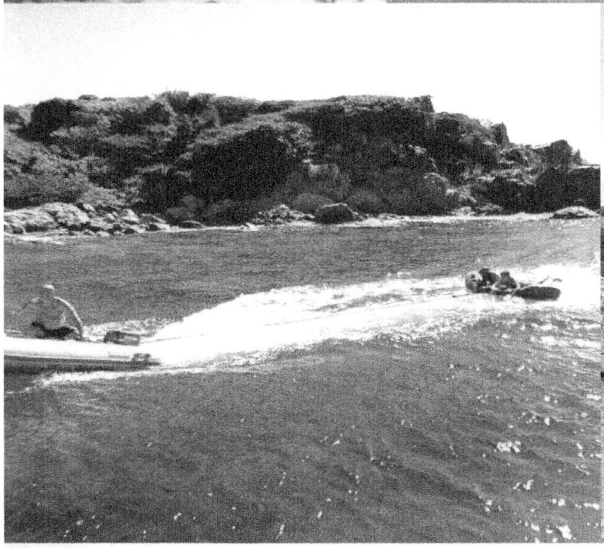
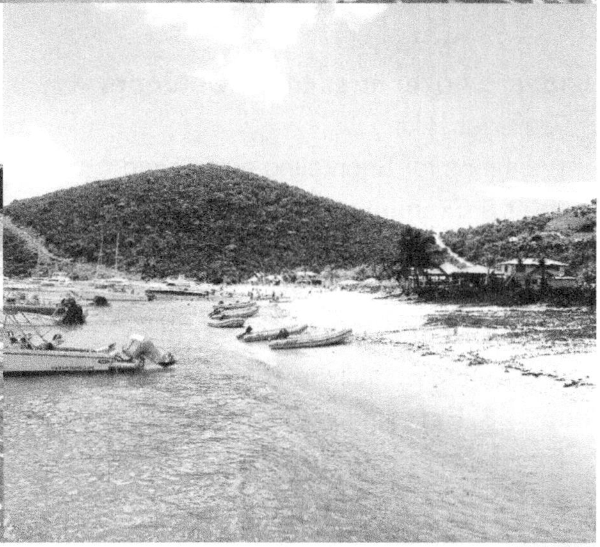
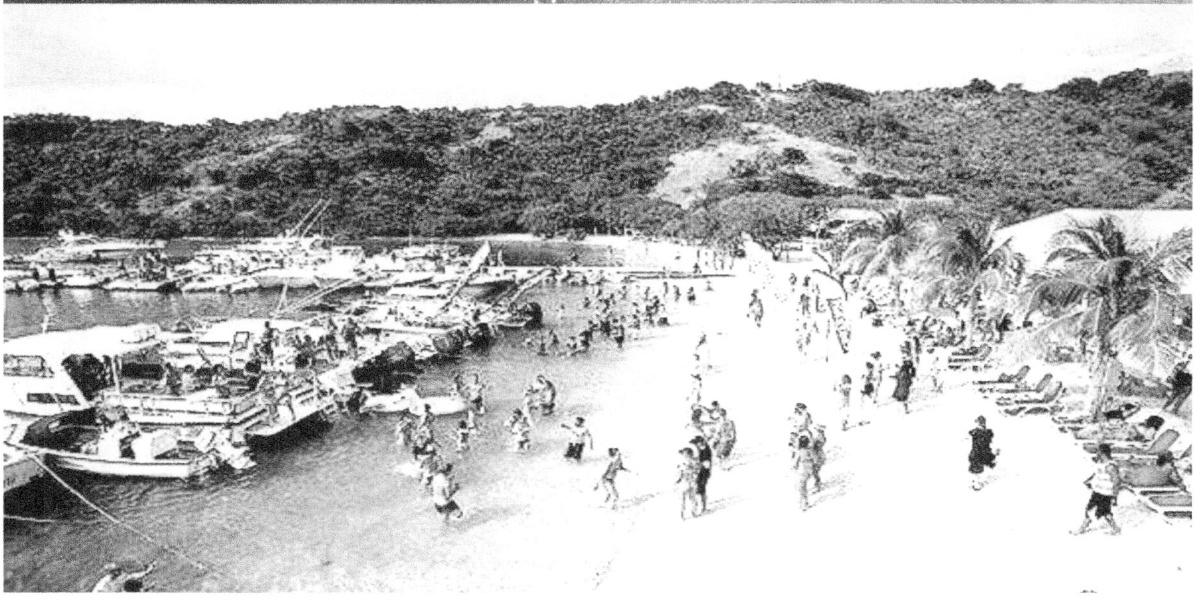

Table of Content

Chapter 1. Overview — 5
   An Outline of St. John — 5
   Why Go to St. John? — 6

Chapter 2. How to Get There and Around — 8
   Options for Transportation — 8
   Getting Around the Island — 19

Chapter 3. Places to Stay — 25
   Hotels and Resorts — 25
   Vacation Rentals — 30

Chapter 4. The Best Beaches — 34
   The Trunk Bay — 34

Chapter 5. Adventures in the Outdoors — 49
   Trails for Hiking — 49
   Locations for Snorkeling and Diving — 53

Chapter 6. Examining the National Park of the Virgin Islands — 58
   Must-See Locations — 58
   Conservation and Wildlife — 62

Chapter 7. Regional Food and Dining — 67
   Top Dining Establishments — 67

Chapter 8. Experiences with Culture — 71
   Events and Festivals — 71
   Regional Crafts and Art — 73

Chapter 9. Insider Advice — 76
   The Best Times to Go — 76
   Advice for Eco-Friendly Travel — 79

Chapter 10. Useful Information — 83
   Itineraries — 83
   Essentials for Traveling — 88
   Etiquette and Safety — 92

Vela Vista

St John
Virgin Island with
wildlife & beaches

Bay Frst Rd

Calvert C.

St. John

Scan the QR code

1. Open Camera: Launch your smartphone's camera app.
2. Position QR Code: Place the QR code within the camera's viewfinder.
3. Hold Steady: Keep the device steady for the camera to focus.
4. Wait for Scan: Wait for the code to be recognized.
5. Tap Notification: Follow the prompt to access the content.

Chapter 1. Overview

An Outline of St. John

Welcome to St. John, the tiniest but most charming of the U.S. islands. Picture yourself arriving on an island where time seems to stand still, the sea glistens like liquid sapphire, and the beauty of nature is the main attraction. Virgin Islands. In contrast to its busy neighbors, St. Thomas and St. Croix, St. John provides a tranquil haven where unspoiled scenery and genuine island charm flourish.

I was astounded by the island's sense of purity and peace when I arrived. St. John is a nature lover's paradise, with two-thirds of its territory protected by the Virgin Islands National Park. Bright coral reefs are teeming with marine life just waiting to be discovered, while verdant hills tumble into turquoise waters. Every sunrise sets the mood for a day of exploration and leisure by painting the sky in shades of pink and gold.

The island's rich cultural heritage and sense of community are what make St. John unique, in addition to its picture-perfect beaches like Cinnamon Bay and Trunk Bay. Hidden along hiking paths are relics from sugar plantations that provide insights into a complicated past, and amiable residents tell tales of joy and resiliency.

St. John offers something for everyone, whether you're a beach lover looking for hidden coves, an adventurous keen to walk the untamed Ram Head Trail, or a foodie ready to sample Caribbean cuisine. It's an experience that stays with you long after your vacation is over, not merely a place to visit.

Why Go to St. John?

St. John is more than simply a place to visit; it's a haven for anyone looking for the ideal fusion of unspoiled landscapes, outdoor activities, and genuine island culture. St. John offers an experience that will never be forgotten, whether your goal is to relax on immaculate beaches, explore verdant tropical forests, or enjoy the relaxed Caribbean way of life.

Beautiful Beaches and Stunningly Clear Waters

- Some of the world's most stunning beaches may be found at St. John. Trunk Bay is like entering paradise with its fine white beach and underwater snorkeling trail. Maho Bay and Salt Pond Bay provide peaceful locations ideal for rest or a cool swim for a more private getaway. Even before you put on your snorkeling equipment, you may view a variety of marine life in the island's crystal-clear waters.

Unrivaled Natural Beauty

- St. John features unspoiled vistas that are uncommon in today's world, with two-thirds of the island protected as part of the Virgin Islands National Park. Through thick forests, hiking routes lead to sweeping vistas, secluded coves, and the remains of a former sugar mill. You will be in awe of the island's natural splendor whether you are hiking the Reef Bay Trail or watching the sunset from Ram Head.

A Refuge for Exploration

- St. John is an outdoor enthusiast's paradise, offering everything from snorkeling over vibrant coral reefs to paddleboarding in serene harbors. While the island's waterways entice you with chances for kayaking, sailing, and diving, its hiking paths are suitable for hikers of all skill levels. There is a new experience waiting to be discovered around every corner in St. John.

Local Charm and a Rich History

- The history of St. John is just as fascinating as its natural beauty. The island's colonial past is recounted by the ruins of Danish sugar plantations, and its cultural legacy is preserved through regional customs and celebrations. Visitors are made to feel at home by the kind and hospitable people, who share stories, food, and island traditions.

A Calm Retreat

- In contrast to the more crowded nearby islands, St. John provides a peaceful, pristine haven. Because there isn't an airport or a cruise ship pier, the island is quiet and uncrowded. It's the ideal location for reestablishing a connection with nature and escaping the bustle of everyday life.

St. John is a place that will stick with you long after you leave, whether you're there for the amazing scenery, outdoor activities, or just to unwind in the Caribbean heat. It's a location to fall in love, not just a place to go.

Chapter 2. How to Get There and Around

Options for Transportation

Traveling by Air to St. John

Because St. John lacks an airport of its own, tourists must fly into neighboring St. Thomas' Cyril E. King Airport (STT) and then take a ferry or private boat to St. John. Even though there are several stages involved, the trip is easy and is a part of the fun.

Flying to Cyril E. King Airport in St. Thomas (STT)

The closest airport to St. John is Cyril E. King Airport (STT) on St. Thomas.

Airline Options: Major airlines that fly to STT include American Airlines, Delta, JetBlue, Spirit, and United.

The following cities are served by direct flights: Miami, Atlanta, New York, Charlotte, and Dallas.

The estimated cost of the flight:

From the United States. East Coast: $250 to $500 total

from the United States. Midwest: $400 to $700 total

from the United States. West Coast: round-trip: $600–$900

Seasonal Pricing: Flights are less expensive in the off-season (May–November) and more expensive during the busiest travel months (December–April).

From St. John to Cyril E. King Airport

Ferry Terminal Taxis:

Outside the airport, taxis are easily accessible.

- It takes about 30 to 40 minutes to get to the Red Hook Ferry Terminal (East End of St. Thomas) for $15 to $20 per person.
- ~$8–$10 per passenger; approximately 10–15 minutes to Charlotte Amalie Ferry Terminal (nearer to the airport).

Transportation to St. John:

Cruz Bay (St. John) to Red Hook:

Hourly is the frequency.

- About 15 to 20 minutes in length
- A one-way ticket is about $6 per passenger, plus about $4 for luggage.

- Cruz Bay (St. John) to Charlotte Amalie:
- Frequency: Few daily departures
- About thirty to forty-five minutes
- Price: around $12 per person, one way

Private Transfers:

- Private boat transports or water taxis provide a customized and adaptable experience.
- Approximately $75 to $125 per person

Travel Advice and Important Details

- **U.S. Citizens**: While a government-issued ID is advised, a passport is not necessary for travel from the United States.

- **International Travelers**: Depending on your nationality, you may need a U.S. visa in addition to a valid passport.

- **Travel Insurance**: Think about getting travel insurance, particularly from June to November when hurricanes are common.

- **Ferry Luggage Fees**: Taking more than one suitcase on a ferry may incur additional costs.

- **Evening Arrivals**: Since the last ferry from Red Hook usually departs at 11:00 PM, make sure your flight coincides with ferry timings.

- **Cash**: Since ferries and taxis frequently do not take credit cards, bring modest cash.

By doing these actions, you'll discover that arriving at St. John is the start of your journey rather than only a means to an end. The stunning ferry voyage and picturesque cab journeys prepare you for the island's natural splendor.

Taking the Ferry to St. John

The most popular way for tourists to get to St. John is by ferry because the island lacks an airport. Ferries offer a picturesque, tranquil journey over the Caribbean's azure waters, and they depart from St. Thomas, the closest adjacent island. A thorough guide to ferry travel to St. John is provided below, complete with departure locations, timetables, prices, and advice.

Points of departure for Ferries on St. Thomas

East End of St. Thomas's Red Hook Ferry Terminal:

Red Hook's proximity to St. John makes it the most popular route because it's the closest terminus to St. John.

It takes about 15 to 20 minutes to go to Cruz Bay (St. John).

Frequency: Usually operating from 6:00 AM to 11:00 PM, ferries run every hour.

It costs about $6 per person (one trip), plus an extra $4 for each bag.

How to Get There:

From Cyril E. King Airport, take a taxi for about $15 to $20 per person (30 to 40 minutes).

By **rental car**: Red Hook offers parking, although there isn't much room.

Nearer to the airport is the Charlotte Amalie Ferry Terminal:

Close to St. John: This terminal, which is close to Cyril E. King Airport, provides a practical choice for travelers coming by plane.

It takes about 35 to 45 minutes to get to Cruz Bay (St. John).

Frequency: Check schedules ahead of time; limited daily departures.

Cost: about $12 per person (one trip); there is an extra $4 for each bag.

How to Get There:

From Cyril E. King Airport, take a taxi for about $8 to $10 per person (10 to 15 minutes).

Custom water taxis and private marinas:

Customized ferry services are provided by private businesses from several St. Thomas marinas.

Price: around $75 to $125 per person, or a fixed price for small parties.

Benefits include increased privacy, direct service to your location, and flexible timings.

Reservations: Make reservations in advance with water taxi companies such as St. John Water Taxi or Dolphin Water Taxi.

St. John Ferry Terminals

Terminal at Cruz Bay:

Cruz Bay, the major town of St. John, is where all boats from St. Thomas arrive.

Because of its convenient location, the port offers easy access to lodging, rental cars, and taxis for island exploration.

Ferry Timetables

Cruz Bay to Red Hook:

- Ferry first: about 6:00 AM
- Ferry last: at 11:00 p.m.
- Frequency: Hourly.

Amalie Charlotte to Cruz Bay:

- Ferry 1: approximately 9:00 AM
- Ferry last: at 5:30 p.m.
- Frequency: two to three daily departures.

Variations in Holidays:

Holidays and inclement weather can cause schedule changes. Consult the ferry operators in advance.

Advice for Getting on the Ferry

Arrive Early: In order to get tickets and handle luggage, arrive at least thirty minutes prior to departure, particularly during periods of high travel demand.

Cash Payments: Bring modest money for tickets and luggage fees, as many ferry operators only accept cash.

Luggage handling: If you have more or larger luggage, be ready to spend more.

Ferry Transfers: Because there are fewer and more costly auto ferries to St. John if you are renting a car on St. Thomas, park at the ferry station or leave the car behind.

Sea situations: Ferries run in most weather situations, although in stormy or choppy seas, excursions may be canceled or postponed.

Option for Car Ferries

Car ferries, sometimes known as barge ferries, are available for passengers with a car between Red Hook and Enighed Pond, which is located immediately south of Cruz Bay.

Cost: around $50 to $65 per car (round-trip), plus an additional $3 per passenger.

4–6 departures per day is the frequency.

About twenty to twenty-five minutes.

Booking: Since tickets are sold on a first-come, first-served basis, and space is limited, arrive early.

Why Opt for the Ferry?

Cost-effective and picturesque: Ferries offer stunning views of the Caribbean seas at an affordable price.

Convenient: Red Hook's regular timings make preparation simple.

Eco-Friendly: Compared to private charters or water taxis, shared ferries have a smaller environmental impact.

A fun and beautiful way to get to know the island is by ferry to St. John. This means of transportation guarantees a smooth and unforgettable trip to your tropical paradise, whether you opt for a vehicle ferry, a private water taxi, or a regular passenger ferry.

Taking the Bus to St. John

Buses can be a useful form of transportation when commuting from neighboring locations like St. Thomas or inside the United States, even though there are no direct buses to St. John because of its island position. Virgin Islands. This section will discuss the use of buses in your trip to St. John, especially when paired with other forms of transportation like taxis or ferries.

Taking the Bus in St. Thomas

Bus services can assist you in getting to the ferry terminals that connect to St. John if you're flying into St. Thomas. The role of buses in the process is as follows:

The public bus system in St. Thomas:

St. Thomas's public bus system offers reasonably priced transit between the island's main hubs, such as the ferry ports and the airport.

Fares: Usually between $1 and $2 per person, it's a cost-effective way to travel.

Bus Routes: Red Hook, Charlotte Amalie (the capital), and other important locations are served by public buses that go across St. Thomas.

Buses operate on a regular basis, although schedules might change and they can get crowded during the busiest travel seasons.

Duration: A trip from Cyril E. King Airport to Red Hook, where the boat to St. John departs, usually takes 30 to 40 minutes, depending on traffic.

Shuttle buses and private bus services

Several private businesses and lodging establishments in St. Thomas provide shuttle bus services that can transport you to the ferry ports if you'd rather take the easier and more direct route:

Shuttle Services for Hotels:

Shuttle services to the major ferry terminals, especially Red Hook, are offered by a number of St. Thomas hotels and resorts.

Cost: Depending on the distance and whether it's a shared or private shuttle, shuttle services can cost anywhere from $10 to $25 per person.

Reservation: Hotel shuttle services frequently require reservations, especially during peak travel times.

Private Shuttle Services:

On St. Thomas, private shuttle services are also available, offering a more individualized and straightforward path to the ferry terminals.

Cost: Flat fees for small groups or $25 to $50 per person are possible options for private shuttle services.

Reservation: It is advised to reserve a private shuttle well in advance, particularly if you have a busy schedule or are traveling in a group.

Benefits: You will be picked up straight from your lodging and dropped off at the ferry terminal by these shuttles, which may provide door-to-door service.

Getting to the Ferry Terminals via Bus

Buses are necessary to get to the ferry terminals in St. Thomas, even though they don't go straight to St. John. St. John may be reached from two major ferry terminals:

Ferry Terminal in Red Hook:

Red Hook, the busiest ferry station for passengers going to St. John, is a regular stop for public buses and shuttle services.

Cruz Bay on St. John can be reached by passenger ferry from here in about 15 to 20 minutes.

Ferry Terminal at Charlotte Amalie:

This terminal, which is close to Cyril E. King Airport, provides ferries to St. John on a more constrained timetable. You can also get here via private shuttle or public transport.

Combining Ferry and Bus Transportation

To get to St. John, most tourists will need to take a combination of bus and ferry transportation:

- **Step 1:** Take a bus to a ferry station in St. Thomas from Cyril E. King Airport (or your hotel).

- Bus travel from the airport to Red Hook should take 30 to 40 minutes.

- **Step 2:** Depending on your departure location, the ferry voyage to Cruz Bay on St. John from the ferry station takes between 15 to 45 minutes.

- To get to your lodging or explore St. John, you can take a cab or hire a car from Cruz Bay.

Benefits of Bus Transportation

- **Reasonably priced**: Bus tickets are reasonably priced, which makes this a cost-effective choice for tourists, especially if you're going alone or in a small group.

- **Scenic Routes**: When passing through the hills and along the shore, the bus rides on St. Thomas can provide beautiful views of the island.

- **Local Experience**: You can engage with people and get a taste of daily life on St. Thomas by taking the bus.

The Difficulties of Bus Travel

- **Restricted Flexibility**: You might need to carefully schedule your time because public buses do not run as frequently as private shuttles or cabs.

- **No Direct Access to St. John**: You will still need to use a ferry to go to the island because there are no buses that go there directly.

Potential Delays: Especially during busy times or tourist seasons, traffic or packed circumstances may cause delays for public buses.

Other Ways to Get to St. John

Even while buses might be a useful element of your trip, you should think about the other options for transportation:

- **Taxi Services:** Taxis are widely available in St. Thomas and can provide a more convenient and direct means of transportation to ferry terminals and other locations.

- **Rental Cars:** Before taking the boat to St. John, you can tour St. Thomas at your own speed if you're more of an independent person.

- **Private Water Taxis**: You can choose a private water taxi to transport you straight to St. John from different locations in St. Thomas for a more upscale and expedient journey.

Buses are an important part of your travel schedule if you're starting your voyage on St. Thomas, even though they don't go directly to St. John. Buses will assist you in getting throughout the island to the ferry terminals, where you can continue your trip to St. John, whether you choose to use public transportation or private shuttle services. Combining bus and ferry travel offers a simple, scenic, and reasonably priced option to get to the island.

How to Drive to St. John

You can drive to St. John by first going to St. Thomas and then catching the boat to St. John, even though St. John is an island without its airport. Here are some tips for driving to St. John, including where to park, where to drive, and what to expect along the trip.

Traveling by car to St. Thomas

Arrival at St. Thomas's Cyril E. King Airport:

- **Location**: The airport is a ten to fifteen-minute drive from the capital, Charlotte Amalie, on the southern coast of St. Thomas.

- **Automobile Rentals**: Cyril E. King Airport is home to several automobile rental companies. You can rent a car when you get there or reserve one in advance. Before taking the ferry, renting a car is a common way to move around the island.

- **Cost**: Depending on the type of vehicle and the rental business, daily rental car rates can vary from $40 to $100.

- **Insurance**: Recognize that rental cars in the United States. It's crucial to inquire about coverage from your rental provider because the Virgin Islands can need extra insurance.

Driving to the Ferry Terminal from the Airport:

East End of St. Thomas's Red Hook Ferry Terminal:

- It takes roughly 30 to 40 minutes to drive (10 to 15 miles, depending on traffic) from the airport.

- **Parking**: The Red Hook Ferry Terminal has a small amount of parking accessible. Parking spots tend to fill up fast during busy seasons, and daily rates range from $10 to $20.

- Nearer to the airport is the Charlotte Amalie Ferry Terminal:

- About ten to fifteen minutes by automobile (5 kilometers) from the airport.

- Parking is often less expensive than at Red Hook, but there isn't much of it close to the Charlotte Amalie Ferry Terminal. Make sure to check availability in advance, particularly during periods when tourism is at its highest.

Traveling to St. John via Ferry

You must take a ferry to St. John after driving to one of the ferry ports in St. Thomas. For ferry services, there are two primary choices:

Ferries for passengers:

Cruz Bay (St. John) to Red Hook:

- Travel time: fifteen to twenty minutes.
- One-way cost: about $6 per person.
- Frequency: From early dawn till late evening, ferries depart roughly every hour.
- The first ferry typically leaves around 6:00 AM, while the last one leaves at 11:00 PM.
- Charlotte Amalie to St. John's Cruz Bay:
- It takes 35 to 45 minutes to travel.
- **Price**: about $12 per person, one way.
- **Frequency**: Two to three ferries every day, fewer departures than Red Hook.

Automobile Ferries:

- You can take a vehicle ferry from Red Hook to St. John if you're driving a rented car.
- Car ferries often depart four to six times a day.
- About 20 to 25 minutes is the estimated travel time.
- Cost: around $50 to $65 per car (round-trip), plus an additional $3 to $4 per passenger.
- **Booking**: To guarantee a position for your car, it is recommended to arrive early as car ferry tickets are frequently sold on a first-come, first-served basis.

St. John parking

There are several parking choices available once you get to Cruz Bay on St. John:

- **Public Parking Lots**: The Cruz Bay ferry port is next to a number of public parking lots. It costs about $5 to $10 per day to park here.
- **Hotel Parking**: Free or reduced parking may be available to visitors staying at a resort or hotel. Asking questions at the time of booking is always preferable.
- **Street Parking**: There is a limited amount of street parking available, however, abide by the rules to avoid fines.

Getting Around St. John by Car

When you get to St. John, you can drive around the island to see all of its sights. What you should know about driving on St. John is as follows:

Road Conditions: St. John's roads are typically winding and narrow. A four-wheel-drive vehicle is advised for exploring several places because some of them are unpaved, particularly in the island's more isolated regions.

Because St. John is a small island, there is typically little traffic. However, roads around well-known locations like Cruz Bay, Trunk Bay, and Cinnamon Bay may get busier during the busiest travel seasons, particularly during the winter.

Driving Advice: As is common in the United States, drive on the left side of the road in St. John. Virgin Islands. Keep an eye out for wildlife and pedestrians, especially in more remote or rural regions.

Additional Advice for Traveling to St. John

- Although driving on St. Thomas is easy, some parts of St. John might need to be navigated, therefore bring a map or GPS. To travel around, think about utilizing a GPS or a map program on your phone.

- **Avoid the Need for a Car on St. John**: Since many attractions are reachable by taxi or foot, you might not need a car on St. John if you intend to stay in Cruz Bay and take advantage of the beaches and treks.

- **St. John Car Rentals**: While renting a car directly on St. John is feasible, availability may be restricted and costs may be higher. Renting a car on St. Thomas and taking the boat over is usually more economical.

Driving to St. Thomas and then taking a boat is the first step in getting to St. John by vehicle. This procedure offers a flexible and picturesque method to get to the island, but it does involve some organization, particularly about parking and ferry timetables. Having a car allows you to explore St. John at your leisure, whether you're driving from the airport or renting one to get around the island after you get there.

Getting Around the Island

Walking, Bicycling, Driving, Busing, and Boating in St. John

With its breathtaking beaches, untamed scenery, and relaxed vibe, St. John provides a variety of ways to explore the island. Every kind of transportation, including walking, bicycling, driving, and public transportation, delivers a different experience. Whether you're driving to the best overlooks, cycling through peaceful roads, trekking along picturesque paths, or using public transportation, this is a thorough guide to getting around the island.

Walking Around St. John's Beaches and Trails

If you want to get a close-up look at St. John's natural splendor, walking is one of the best ways to see the city. Best experienced on foot, the island offers a vast network of hiking routes, beautiful beaches, and wildlife reserves.

Well-liked Paths for Hiking:

- The Lind Point walk is a somewhat easy walk that leads to stunning beaches including Salomon Bay and Honeymoon Beach and connects Cruz Bay with the Virgin Islands National Park. The Caribbean Sea may be seen from the well-kept trail.

- **Reef Bay Trail**: This journey, which is more difficult, leads past old petroglyphs, through tropical rainforest, and concludes at the breathtaking Reef Bay Beach. Discover the history of St. John on this trip, which includes historic ruins and undiscovered waterfalls.

- The Cinnamon Bay Trail is a quick, picturesque hike that begins close to Cinnamon Bay Beach and takes in the views of the surrounding woodland and coastline.

Beaches:

- **Trunk Bay**: Known for its underwater snorkeling trail, this beach is among St. John's most well-known. It is perfect for a leisurely beach day because it is conveniently located near the parking lot.

- **Hawksnest Beach**: Less crowded than Trunk Bay, this beach is calmer and excellent for strolling along the shore.

Exploring Cruz Bay on Foot:

- Cruz Bay, the main settlement on the island, is small and simple to walk around. The ferry pier is only a short stroll from stores, eateries, and art galleries. It's a fantastic place to start if you want to take your time touring the island on foot.

Shoes:

- Comfortable, sturdy shoes are crucial, particularly when trekking. The terrain on many of the routes is rough and rocky. Invest in appropriate hiking shoes or sandals with strong traction if you intend to hike a lot.

Riding a Bicycle: A Beautiful Tour of St. John

Cycling around St. John is a fun way to take in the island's rugged landscape and seaside routes. With its peaceful lanes and a few bike rental stores, St. John is a reasonably bike-friendly city. It's best to be ready for some difficult climbs because the terrain might be mountainous.

Rental Bicycles:

- Mountain bikes, beach cruisers, and electric bikes for a smoother ride are among the bikes available for rent at a number of stores in Cruz Bay and other locations throughout the island. Usually, rates fall between $25 and $50 per day.

Well-liked Cycling Paths:

- **Cruz Bay to Coral Bay**: You travel over beautiful coastal roads that offer views of the ocean and verdant surroundings. There are some hilly parts along the about 10-mile one-way bike.

- **North Shore Road**: This road connects a number of beaches and hiking trails, and it gives stunning views of the coastline. The North Shore is known for its undulating hills, so be ready for some uphill stretches.

Security:

- When riding on St. John's twisting, narrow roads, notably North Shore Road, use caution and wear a helmet (which is typically included with rentals).

- Given how strong the sun can be, pack plenty of water and sunscreen.

Electric bicycles:

- Electric bikes are a fantastic choice for anyone who wants a smoother ride. These bikes make uphill climbs easier by offering help during pedaling. They are particularly helpful for negotiating the high hills on the island.

Driving: Getting Around St. John's Roads

- If you want to visit some of the most isolated beaches and hiking paths on St. John, driving allows you the freedom to see the island at your speed. Despite the island's modest size, it is important to drive carefully because the roads can be steep and narrow.

Conditions of the Road:

- Although paved, St. John's principal roadways are sometimes winding and narrow. If you intend to venture off the main route, a four-wheel-drive vehicle is advised because certain roads, especially in the more rural parts, are unpaved and can be bumpy.

- As in the majority of the United States, driving on the left. Driving on the left side of the road is the norm in the Virgin Islands. If you're traveling from the United States or another nation where right-side driving is practiced, be mindful of this.

Well-traveled routes and locations:

- The primary route that connects Cruz Bay with Coral Bay on the island is Centerline Road. It serves as the main means of transportation between the island's two halves.

- Access to some of St. John's most stunning beaches, such as Trunk Bay and Cinnamon Bay, is made possible by the North Shore Road, which traces the northern shoreline.

- The old Annaberg Plantation ruins can be reached via the short yet picturesque Annaberg Plantation Road.

Parking

- Although parking is usually available in Cruz Bay and at well-known beaches like Trunk Bay, it can fill up fast during busy times. To guarantee a seat, be ready to arrive early, particularly during the busiest times of the year (December to April).

- Due to parking restrictions at several isolated beaches and hiking locations, a four-wheel-drive vehicle is useful for getting to these locations.

Automobile Rentals:

Although most tourists hire in St. Thomas and take their cars over on the car ferry, you can rent a car on St. John. There aren't many rental automobiles available in St. John, so reservations should be made well in advance.

By Bus: St. John's Public Transportation

- Although there are buses to move across the island and to important locations like Cruz Bay, Coral Bay, and the ferry terminals, St. John's public transportation system is not as comprehensive as those on larger islands.

The public bus system

- Although buses can transport you from the ferry terminals to Cruz Bay and surrounding regions, the public bus system primarily serves St. Thomas. If you're staying in St. Thomas, you can use this service to move around.

- **Fees**: The average bus ticket is between $1 and $2 per passenger. The bus is a reasonably priced yet rather constrained way to get around St. John.

Shuttle Services:

- Shuttle services to the ferry ports are offered by several St. Thomas hotels and resorts. To go to the ferry terminals in St. Thomas, where you'll board the ferry to St. John, these can be a practical choice.

By Boat: Getting Around St. John by Water

- Because of St. John's remote location, boat travel is necessary in some areas of the island. The sea is essential for island transportation, whether you're traveling by ferry, renting a private boat, or engaging in water sports.

Ferries

- **Ferries for Passengers**: Ferries are the most popular means of transportation between St. Thomas and St. John. The trip takes 15 to 45 minutes, and there are frequent ferries from Red Hook and Charlotte Amalie.

- **Car Ferries**: You can go from Red Hook to St. John via car ferry if you have leased a vehicle on St. Thomas. The trip takes roughly twenty to twenty-five minutes, and the automobile ferry runs many times a day.

Charters for Private Boats:

Exploring St. John and the neighboring islands in style can be achieved by renting a private boat or yacht. For private island-hopping tours, snorkeling, and day excursions, boat charters are offered.

Cost: Depending on the boat's size and the services offered, private charters can cost anywhere from $500 to $1,500+ per day.

Water Taxis:

From St. Thomas to St. John, water taxis are offered for customers seeking a more direct and customized trip. They are the best option for people who wish to avoid the boat throng because they are quicker and frequently more private.

Walking along picturesque paths, riding along coastal roads, driving through verdant forests, or taking a ferry to neighboring islands are just a few of the ways to experience St. John's breathtaking scenery. You can select the most appropriate form of transportation based on your tastes and the degree of adventure you're looking for. Every mode of transportation—foot, bike, vehicle, bus, or boat—offers a different approach to take in St. John's splendor and allure.

Chapter 3. Places to Stay

Hotels and Resorts

Exquisite Resorts

The Caneel Bay Resort

Located in the Virgin Islands National Park, Caneel Bay Resort is one of St. John's most recognizable upscale resorts. The resort features immaculate homes and cottages on the beach, encircled by beautiful tropical vegetation.

Caneel Bay is well-known for its dedication to sustainability and its breathtaking natural surroundings, making it a popular destination for tourists looking for luxury amenities, adventure, and relaxation.

What to anticipate:

- Large villas on the hillside and by the beach.
- Opportunities for fine dining with views of the water.
- Water sports and activities include kayaking, paddleboarding, sailing, and snorkeling.
- Full-service health and spa centers.
- Access to several breathtaking beaches, such as Caneel Bay, which is reserved for resort visitors.
- Numerous locations within Virgin Islands National Park offer wildlife views, hiking trails, and nature walks.

How to Get There:

- Ferries from St. Thomas to Cruz Bay provide access to Caneel Bay Resort, which is then only a short drive or shuttle ride away. As an alternative, visitors can fly straight into St. Thomas, travel to St. John by ferry or cab, and then proceed to the resort.

Price:

- Generally speaking, rates vary from $700 to $1,500+ per night, contingent on the season and type of hotel. Villa and suite rates can differ.

Extra Details:

- Availability may vary as Caneel Bay Resort is currently undergoing renovation following hurricane damage. For updates, it's best to contact the resort.

Villas at The Westin St. John Resort

With a range of amenities to suit both leisure and adventure, the Westin St. John Resort Villas is a luxurious resort with roomy villa rooms. The resort is conveniently close to the island's beaches and activities because it is situated on the shores of Great Cruz Bay.

What to anticipate:

- Villas have private balconies, kitchens, and one, two, or three bedrooms.
- Access to the beach for swimming and relaxing.
- A fitness center, hot baths, and a sizable outdoor pool.
- Both foreign and local cuisines are served at the on-site dining options.
- Availability of water sports, such as sailing, paddleboarding, kayaking, and snorkeling.
- Spa with full services for rest and renewal.

How to Get There:

- Cruz Bay is home to the Westin St. John Resort Villas. From Red Hook (St. Thomas) or Charlotte Amalie, visitors can take a ferry to Cruz Bay, after which they can take a taxi to the resort. As an alternative, visitors can go from St. Thomas by vehicle ferry, or private boat.

Price:

- Generally speaking, rates vary from $500 to $1,200 a night, contingent on the season, size of the villa, and amenities. Discounted rates can be available for extended stays.

Extra Details:

- With activities for all ages, the Westin St. John Resort Villas provides a more family-friendly setting than other upscale properties on the island.

Hotels in Boutiques

Resort at Gallows Point

Situated in Cruz Bay, Gallows Point Resort is a boutique resort with breathtaking views of the Caribbean Sea and convenient access to eateries, retail establishments, and beaches. The resort offers a quiet and intimate experience with its opulent rooms and cottages.

What to anticipate:

- Large, independent suites with individual balconies, kitchens, and views of the ocean.
- Remote but still close to Cruz Bay's restaurants and retail establishments.
- Water activities and snorkeling options are available at this exclusive seaside location.
- Hot tub and heated outdoor pool.
- Concierge services for reservations and bookings of excursions are available on-site.

How to Get There:

- The Cruz Bay ferry dock is within a short distance from Gallows Point Resort. Visitors can stroll or take a quick cab ride to the resort after taking a ferry from St. Thomas to Cruz Bay.

Price:

- The cost per night varies from $450 to $800 based on the facilities, season, and size of the unit.

Extra Details:

Known for its tranquil ambiance, Gallows Point Resort is a great option for honeymooners and couples.

Lindholm Estate

- Situated atop a hill with a view of Cruz Bay, the Estate Lindholm is a small, boutique hotel. It offers well-appointed rooms with views of the bay and surrounding surroundings, making it a more private and tranquil experience.

What to anticipate:

- Many of the well-decorated suites with their patios have breathtaking views of the ocean.
- Gorgeously designed grounds give the feel of a tropical garden.
- Free continental breakfast, whirlpool, and outdoor pool access.
- The ferry station, restaurants, and stores in Cruz Bay are all within walking distance.
- Customized concierge services to help with tour and activity reservations.

How to Get There:

- Cruz Bay is a short stroll or taxi ride away from the Estate Lindholm. From the ferry terminal, visitors may conveniently reach the hotel after arriving on St. John via ferry.

Price:

- The normal nightly rate is between $300 and $600, depending on the time of year and type of hotel.

Extra Details:

- The adults-only Estate Lindholm is a great place for couples or anybody looking for a peaceful, romantic retreat.

Hotels in the Mid-Range

The St. John Inn

A short stroll from the ferry port, the St. John Inn is a mid-range hotel in Cruz Bay that provides a comfortable and reasonably priced stay. For those seeking a simple, practical starting point for exploring the island, the inn is perfect.

What to anticipate:

- Basic facilities like TV, air conditioning, and private toilets are provided in tidy, uncomplicated rooms.
- Access to neighboring beaches and hiking trails, as well as an outdoor pool.
- On-site parking and a complimentary continental breakfast are provided.
- Close to the eateries, bars, and stores in Cruz Bay.

How to Get There:

- A short stroll from the boat station in Cruz Bay. Cruz Bay is reachable by ferry from Red Hook or Charlotte Amalie (St. Thomas).

Price:

- It is a reasonably priced option for tourists on a tight budget, with rates usually ranging from $150 to $250 a night.

Extra Details:

- If you wish to visit St. John on a tight budget without compromising comfort, the St. John Inn is a great option.

The Wharf Suites

- Spacious rooms with kitchenettes and stunning views of Cruz Bay's shoreline are available at rooms at the Wharf. For those seeking a self-catering alternative near the center of the island, this is a fantastic mid-range choice.

What to anticipate:

- Suites with one or two bedrooms, private balconies, kitchens, and views of the waterfront.
- Close to the ferry station, restaurants, and stores in Cruz Bay.
- Parking is available on-site, and concierge services are available for reservations for meals and tours.

How to Get There:

- It is conveniently accessible by foot or a quick cab ride from the dock, and it is only a few minutes from the Cruz Bay ferry port.

Price:

- Generally speaking, rates vary from $200 to $350 a night, contingent on the size of the suite and the season.

Extra Details:

- More space and flexibility for families or groups, perfect for extended stays.

Low-Cost Hotels

Campsite in Cinnamon Bay

Cinnamon Bay Campground, which is part of Virgin Islands National Park, provides a distinctive and reasonably priced option to take in the natural splendor of St. John. Eco-friendly tents and simple, rustic bungalows are available at the park.

What to anticipate:

- Eco-cottages and tent camping with simple facilities like mattresses, restrooms, and tiny kitchenettes.
- Cinnamon Bay Beach, perfect for kayaking, swimming, and snorkeling, is just a short stroll away.
- Access to Virgin Islands National Park's historical sites and hiking routes.
- Simple, uncomplicated lodging that is ideal for budget-conscious and nature-loving tourists.

How to Get There:

- From Cruz Bay, it's a 15-minute drive or cab journey. The Cinnamon Bay Campground is also accessible by public bus from Cruz Bay.

Price:

- The normal nightly rate is between $100 and $200, depending on the time of year and the kind of lodging.

Extra Details:

For those who want to experience nature without breaking the bank, Cinnamon Bay is a fantastic option.

Virgin Islands Campsite

Another reasonably priced and environmentally responsible camping choice is Virgin Islands Campground, which is situated inside Virgin Islands National Park. It provides access to stunning beaches and hiking paths, as well as the opportunity to sleep beneath the stars.

What to anticipate:

- Essential facilities, such as picnic spaces and restrooms, for tent camping.
- A lovely, peaceful setting close to several immaculate beaches and trails.
- Minimalist lodgings that prioritize sustainability and outdoor lifestyle.

How to Get There:

- Accessible by public bus or a quick cab trip from Cruz Bay.

Price:

- Rates vary by season and camping type, ranging from $50 to $150 per night.

Extra Details:

- Perfect for outdoor-loving adventurers who don't mind simple, primitive living arrangements.

This extensive list offers a range of lodging options to meet various spending limits and tastes, guaranteeing that guests will discover the perfect place to stay in St. John.

Vacation Rentals

For visitors looking for a more individualized, cozy, and homey stay on St. John, vacation rentals are a well-liked and adaptable lodging choice. Vacation rentals have something to offer any kind of tourist, whether you're searching for a large property for your family or party, an opulent villa with expansive views, or a comfortable one-bedroom cottage. This article offers a thorough analysis of St. John vacation rentals, covering what to anticipate, how to identify the best deals and practical booking advice.

What to anticipate

Numerous Choices:

From compact studios and flats to spacious beachfront villas and private residences, St. John offers a wide range of vacation rental options. There are many different styles available on the island, ranging from opulent homes to primitive huts. There is something to fit your tastes, whether you're looking for a quiet retreat or a home close to well-known beaches.

While some properties maintain their traditional island charm, others are fully furnished and modern. Open room plans, exquisite tropical décor, and outdoor areas that maximize the island's breathtaking natural splendor are all to be expected.

Comfort and Privacy:

The solitude that vacation rentals offer is one of its main advantages. It's perfect for couples, families, or small groups since, unlike hotels or resorts, you can enjoy your own space away from the masses. Additionally, a lot of rentals include completely functional kitchens, so you can prepare your own meals and take advantage of home comforts while visiting.

In addition, many homes have balconies, patios, hot tubs, private pools, and BBQ grills for cooking outside—all of which are ideal for taking advantage of the pleasant island climate.

Special Places:

- Some of the most picturesque and sought-after spots on St. John are home to vacation homes. St. John provides a multitude of varied settings, whether you're searching for homes on the beach, on a hillside with expansive views, or hidden away in a forest or nature reserve.

- Particularly well-liked are rentals close to Virgin Islands National Park, the island's breathtaking beaches, and hiking routes. There are rentals in the center of Cruz Bay that provide easy access to stores, eateries, and ferry terminals if you want to be near the activity.

Value and Cost:

In general, St. John vacation rentals are more affordable than hotels for larger groups and longer stays, particularly for families or friends. The size, location, and degree of luxury of the property can all have a significant impact on the price per night.

Depending on the season and the amenities offered by the facility, the average nightly rate might range from $150 to $1,000 or more. During the busiest time of year, the most opulent villas might even cost more. To get the best bargains, always check prices on several sites and make your reservation in advance.

Where to Look for Vacation Rentals

Well-known websites:

St. John vacation rentals are listed on several websites. Well-known websites consist of:

- Airbnb: A range of lodging options are offered, ranging from luxurious beachfront houses to affordable cottages. You can make an informed choice by reading reviews left by prior visitors.

- Vacation rentals are the focus of Vrbo, which provides a variety of choices, from comfortable flats to larger properties. It's an excellent booking site for families and groups.

- St. John Rental Villas: A neighborhood vacation rental company that focuses on homes in St. John. A variety of high-end villas, cottages, and residences are available.

- Luxury Retreats: Some of the most opulent rentals on the island are available on this site for individuals looking for upscale, private homes.

Local Property Management Firms:

There are local St. John-based property management firms that provide vacation rentals in addition to Internet marketplaces. These businesses usually have a selection of fine residences and villas and are able to offer individualized service and local knowledge.

Cruz Bay Realty, St. John Properties, and Cimmaron St. John are a few examples. These businesses can assist you in finding the ideal properties to suit your requirements.

How to Get to Vacation Rentals and Get There

Reaching Your Rental:

The location of your vacation property will determine how to get there once you get to St. John. Your rental can be readily reached by foot if it's within walking distance or by a quick taxi trip if it's in or close to Cruz Bay.

You might need to rent a car for more remote rentals, particularly those on the north shore or more into Virgin Islands National Park. Directions and even help with transportation arrangements are provided by many vacation rental providers.

Procedure for Check-In:

Vacation rentals usually have a simple check-in procedure. Self-check-in alternatives are available at many properties, where you are given a key code or lockbox code before your arrival.

A property manager may meet you at some upscale vacation rentals, give you a tour, and provide you with useful advice on how to use the facilities.

Advice on Organizing Vacation Rentals

Make Your Reservations Early:

Popular travel destinations include St. John, especially from December to April. It's advisable to reserve your rental a few months in advance to guarantee the greatest selection at affordable prices.

You might be able to find last-minute offers if you're visiting in the off-season (May through November), but availability will be restricted during the busiest months.

Examine reviews:

When choosing a holiday rental, reviews from previous visitors are quite helpful. Check for remarks about the property's location, cleanliness, communication with the host or property manager, and the correctness of the property description. This can help you better understand what to anticipate when you're there.

Inquire About Extra Fees:

Any additional costs, such as cleaning fees, security deposits, or service charges, should be made clear upfront. These expenses should be included in your overall travel budget because they can occasionally be high.

Get in touch with the host:

Ask any questions you may have about the property or its amenities by getting in touch with the manager or owner before making a reservation. Confirming specifics like check-in and check-out times and whether they can offer local recommendations is another chance to do this.

Think About Your Needs:

Consider your particular requirements as well as the size of your group. Look for bigger houses with ample room for everyone if you're vacationing with family or friends. A smaller, cozier cottage can be more suitable for couples or lone travelers. Remember to take into account features like Wi-Fi, air conditioning, and a fully equipped kitchen.

A flexible, cozy, and frequently less expensive option to conventional hotel lodging in St. John is vacation rentals. These residences, which range from comfortable cottages to opulent villas, provide a variety of experiences to fit your preferences and price range. You can find the ideal vacation property that will improve your time on this breathtaking island if you carefully analyze your needs, do your homework, and make your reservation in advance. A vacation rental can be the ideal starting point for your trip to St. John, whether you're searching for a group adventure, a family retreat, or a romantic escape.

Chapter 4. The Best Beaches

The Trunk Bay

Trunk Bay: An Icon of St. John

Situated on St. John in the Virgin Islands National Park, Trunk Bay is one of the most well-known and charming beaches in the Virgin Islands. It provides a calm and picturesque setting for both leisure and exploration and is well-known for its immaculate white sand, glistening waters, and colorful coral reefs.

Things to Investigate:

- Trunk Bay is well-known for its underwater snorkeling trail, which is dotted with signs that describe the different coral and marine life. Both novice and expert snorkelers will love this trail.

- **Marine Life**: Discover colorful coral reefs that are home to rays, sea turtles, tropical fish, and other marine life.

- **Scenic Views**: The beach provides breathtaking views of the nearby islands and is encircled by thick greenery. Particularly around sunrise or sunset, it's an excellent location for photography.

- **Virgin Islands National Park**: The broader Virgin Islands National Park, which includes hiking trails, historic ruins, and scenic views, includes Trunk Bay. Spend some time exploring the neighboring parks and beaches.

- **Trunk Bay Overlook**: This breathtaking view of the bay and surroundings is just a short stroll from the beach. Photographers love this vantage point.

What to anticipate:

- **Pristine White Sand**: The beach is ideal for swimming and tanning because of its gentle, white sand and serene, turquoise waves.

- **Clear Water**: The seas are perfect for swimming and snorkeling because they are so clear. Visibility is frequently more than fifty feet.

- **Calm Ambience**: Despite being a well-known beach, it nevertheless has a calm atmosphere, especially when contrasted with some of the busier beaches.

- **Facilities**: Trunk Bay has amenities like picnic tables, snack bars, showers, and restrooms. Additionally, beach equipment like chairs and snorkels can be rented.

- **Crowds**: Trunk Bay, one of St. John's most visited beaches, can get crowded at the busiest times of the year, particularly on cruise ship days and during the busiest time of year (December to April). Try to go early in the morning or late in the afternoon to avoid the throng.

How to Get There:

- **By Car**: Trunk Bay is reachable from Cruz Bay by a paved road if you have a rental car. The Cruz Bay ferry dock is roughly a fifteen-minute drive away.

- **By Taxi**: St. John is home to several taxis. They can drive you straight to Trunk Bay, and it's customary to schedule a time for the driver to pick you up again.

Scan the QR code

1. Open Camera: Launch your smartphone's camera app.
2. Position QR Code: Place the QR code within the camera's viewfinder.
3. Hold Steady: Keep the device steady for the camera to focus.
4. Wait for Scan: Wait for the code to be recognized.
5. Tap Notification: Follow the prompt to access the content.

- **By Bus:** Cruz Bay offers public bus service, albeit it may not run as frequently. A rental car or taxi is more dependable.

- **By Boat**: Although there isn't a designated dock, Trunk Bay is also reachable by private boat. Visitors typically swim or take a dinghy to get to the beach from boats that anchor offshore.

Price:

- **Entrance Fee:** Since Trunk Bay is a component of Virgin Islands National Park, admission is $5 per person. The cost supports conservation initiatives and park infrastructure upkeep.

- **Costs of Rentals**: For an extra charge, beach chairs, umbrellas, and snorkeling gear can be rented.

- **Parking Fee**: Visitors who drive to the beach must pay a small parking fee, usually $10 per day. It's best to arrive early to guarantee a spot because parking can fill up quickly.

Advice:

- **Arrive Early**: Go early in the morning or late in the afternoon to enjoy the beach uncrowded. While afternoons might be busy, particularly when cruise ships are in dock, mornings are typically calmer.

- Although most establishments in St. John take credit cards, it's still a good idea to keep cash on hand for little purchases, tips, and admission fees.

- **Snorkel Gear**: Although snorkeling equipment can be rented, it's best to bring your own if you have it because it will fit and feel more comfortable. One of Trunk Bay's main draws is the snorkeling trail.

- **Sun Protection**: Bring sunglasses, a hat, and sunscreen because the Virgin Islands can have very strong sun. The beach has very little shade.

- **Respect the Reef**: Remember that Trunk Bay's coral reefs are fragile. When snorkeling, be aware of your effect and avoid touching or stepping on the corals.

- **Hydrate and Snack**: Although the on-site snack bar is available, it can be pricey. If you intend to stay for a long time, think about packing your drinks, snacks, and cooler.

- **Seasonal Considerations**: The dry season (December to April) is when Trunk Bay is most visited. There may be fewer tourists if you go between May and November but be advised that the weather might change at any time.

- **Accessibility**: For people with limited mobility, Trunk Bay is quite accessible. The beach features accessible restrooms and paved pathways from the parking lot to the beach. Nevertheless, there may be mountainous terrain and certain places that are not completely wheelchair accessible.

- **Safety**: Trunk Bay's waters are usually calm, but if you're swimming further out from the coast, watch the current. Always abide by the safety instructions provided and pay attention to any advice given by park employees or lifeguards.

Any visitor to St. John should make time to explore Trunk Bay. This beach has everything you could want, whether you're searching for a laid-back beach day, an undersea adventure, or just a lovely place to enjoy the scenery.

Cinnamon Bay: A Calm Sanctuary

One of St. John's most charming and tranquil beaches is Cinnamon Bay, which is part of Virgin Islands National Park. Cinnamon Bay is well-known for its stunning white beach, serene waters, and a wide variety of activities. It offers a great balance of leisure, excitement, and scenic beauty. For those who prefer a tranquil setting and like to connect with nature while learning a little bit about history, this is the ideal location.

Things to Investigate:

- **Snorkeling**: With so many vibrant coral reefs and marine life, the seas around Cinnamon Bay are ideal for snorkeling. Snorkeling right off the shore is a great way to observe sea turtles, rays, and a variety of fish.

- **Hiking routes**: Within the Virgin Islands National Park, Cinnamon Bay is encircled by a few hiking routes that provide picturesque views of the beach, nearby hills, and coastline. The Reef Bay Trail and the Cinnamon Bay Trail are well-traveled paths that lead to petroglyphs and other fascinating historical sites.

- **Historic Ruins**: A sugar plantation formerly stood on Cinnamon Bay. The plantation's ancient ruins, which include the remnants of an old factory and a slave section, are open to visitors. The area's historical significance is explained with informative signs.

- **Cinnamon Bay Beach:** This St. John beach is less busy than some others, making it a more tranquil and laid-back place to visit. The shaded palm palms provide organic sun protection, and the placid waters are ideal for swimming and relaxing.

- **Water Sports**: You can hire kayaks, paddleboards, and small sailboats in addition to snorkeling. It's a fantastic place for active beachgoers because you can hire equipment for water activities like windsurfing.

What to anticipate:

- **Pristine Beach:** Cinnamon Bay has shallow, clean waters with fine, white sand that are perfect for swimming, wading, or simply lounging in the sun.

- **Quiet seas**: The bay is an excellent place for children and beginners because it is protected and has quiet, clean seas for all kinds of water sports.

- **Less Congested Atmosphere**: Cinnamon Bay is typically calmer and more laid-back than other of St. John's more well-known beaches, particularly on weekdays and in the off-season.

- **Natural Shade**: Although the beach receives a lot of sunlight, it also has natural shade from tall palm trees, which makes it simple to find a cozy location to unwind away from the sun.

- **Facilities**: There are picnic tables, public restrooms, and a small seaside cafe with refreshments and snacks available at the beach. The Cinnamon Bay Campground has cabins, a small supply store, and tent rentals.

Cinnamon Bay

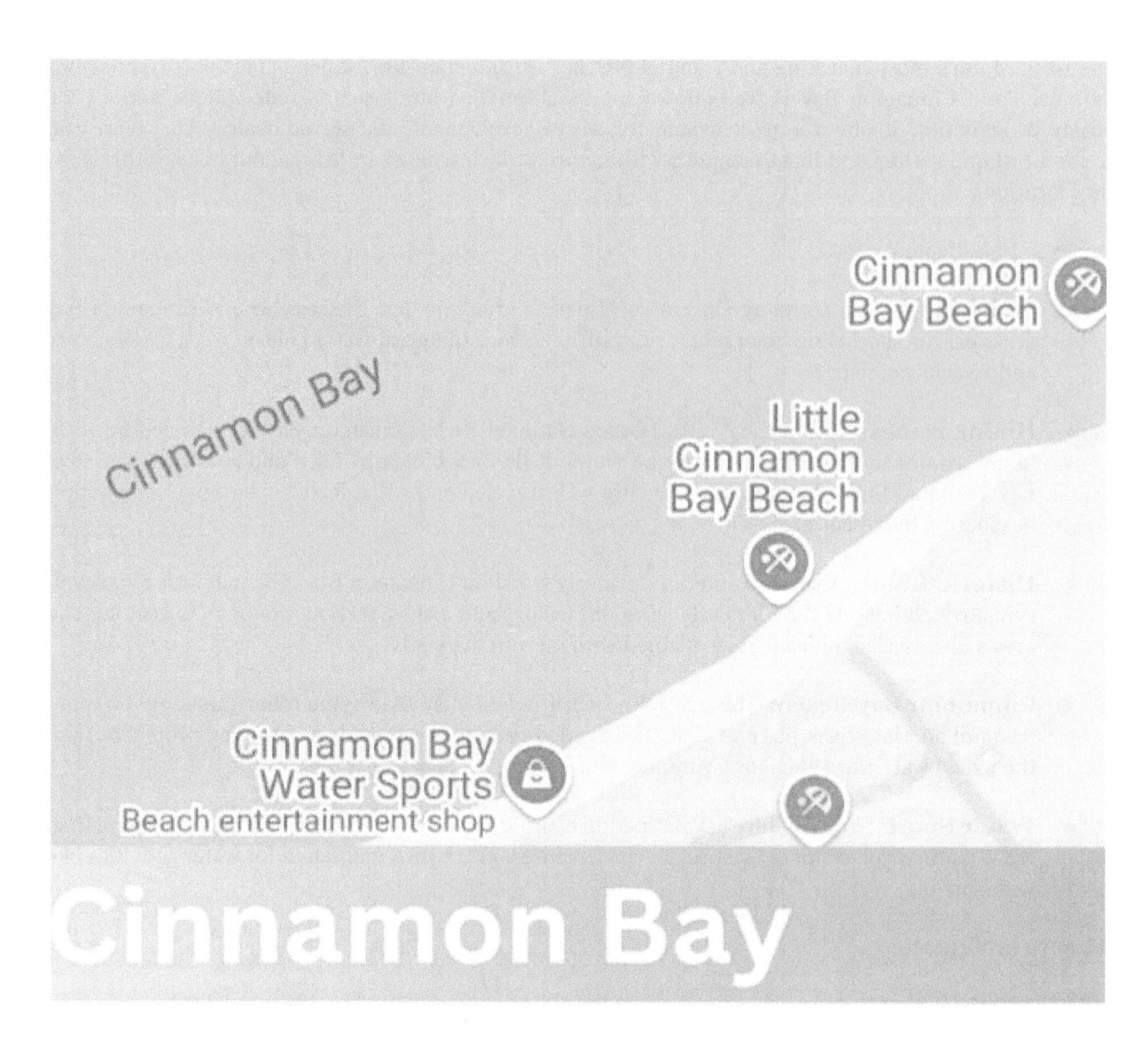

Scan the QR code

1. Open Camera: Launch your smartphone's camera app.
2. Position QR Code: Place the QR code within the camera's viewfinder.
3. Hold Steady: Keep the device steady for the camera to focus.
4. Wait for Scan: Wait for the code to be recognized.
5. Tap Notification: Follow the prompt to access the content.

How to Get There:

- **By Car**: Cinnamon Bay is approximately a fifteen-minute picturesque drive from Cruz Bay. Route 10 will lead you to the beach parking lot, where you will turn into the access road.

- **By Taxi**: You can go straight to the beach in a taxi, which departs from Cruz Bay. Setting up a return pick-up time in advance with the driver is beneficial.

- By Bus: Although it might not be as common as taxis, public transit can get you to Cinnamon Bay. Cruz Bay and the Cinnamon Bay region are connected by a local bus route.

- **By Boat**: You can anchor offshore and take a dinghy to the beach if you're sailing around St. John. But there isn't a designated berth for big ships.

Price:

- Cinnamon Bay is available on the beach without charge, but it is a part of Virgin Islands National Park, which charges $5 per person to enter all park areas.

- Rental costs can vary depending on whether you wish to rent snorkel gear, kayaks, paddleboards, or other equipment. Gear rentals should cost between $20 and $40 per hour.

- **Campsites**: Depending on size and season, cabins at the Cinnamon Bay Campground run from $150 to $300 per night, while tent sites start at about $50.

Advice:

- **Arrive Early or Late**: Cinnamon Bay, like other well-known beaches, can get crowded during the busiest times of the day. If you arrive early in the morning or late in the afternoon, you will be able to enjoy the beach with fewer people.

- **Hire Snorkel Gear**: The seaside store offers snorkeling equipment for hire if you don't have your own. The coral reefs in the area are worth exploring and are great for snorkeling.

- **Stay Hydrated**: If you intend to spend a lot of time on the beach or exploring the nearby trails, it's a good idea to pack your water, even if the beach has a small cafe.

- **Pack Light**: Although there are picnic tables and amenities, it is best to bring a lunch or some snacks because there aren't any full-service eateries right on the beach. Remember to include hats, sunscreen, and proper walking or hiking shoes.

- **Bring Cash**: While many establishments take credit cards, it's always convenient to have cash on hand for minor purchases like snacks or trinkets.

- **Respect Nature:** Make sure to leave no trace as Cinnamon Bay is a part of the Virgin Islands National Park. When snorkeling, don't touch the coral reefs or disturb the creatures.

- **Accessibility**: People with mobility impairments can visit Cinnamon Bay. There are paved pathways that go to the beach area and facilities, and there is a parking lot close by. However, people with mobility impairments might not be able to use some of the hiking routes around the bay.

- **Seasonal Considerations**: December through April, when the weather is ideal for hiking and swimming, is the greatest time of year to visit Cinnamon Bay. The beach is still lovely and less busy in the off-season, though you may experience rain or less consistent weather.

There isn't a lifeguard on duty at Cinnamon Bay, so it's crucial to swim carefully and pay attention to the ocean's conditions.

40

Cinnamon Bay is one of the best beaches on St. John because it provides the ideal harmony of adventure, history, and beauty. It offers guests of all ages an experience they won't soon forget, whether they choose to climb the surrounding trails, explore the underwater world, or simply unwind on the sand.

Maho Bay: A Calm Sanctuary for Those Who Love Nature

One of St. John's most popular beaches, Maho Bay is well-known for its breathtaking scenery, serene waters, and laid-back vibe. Maho Bay, which is part of the Virgin Islands National Park, is a beautiful location for anyone looking for a tranquil getaway in the middle of nature. It's a great place for families, snorkelers, and beach lovers because of its smooth sand, pristine waters, and wealth of animals.

Things to Investigate:

- Maho Bay is one of the best places to go snorkeling. Vibrant coral reefs and a wide variety of marine life, such as sea turtles, rays, and colorful fish, can be found in the bay's serene, shallow waters. The reefs are easily accessible from the beach, which makes it perfect for families and novice snorkelers.

- **Bird Watching**: There is a lot of wildlife, especially birds, in the vicinity of Maho Bay. Look for native animals like herons, pelicans, and the occasional osprey. In addition to offering a peaceful setting, the nearby mangrove habitats are home to a variety of tiny creatures.

- **Paddleboarding and Kayaking**: Maho Bay's calm waters are ideal for paddleboarding and kayaking. For those who would prefer to explore the bay by sea, rentals are offered, offering another viewpoint of the beach and its natural surroundings.

- **Beachcombing**: Maho Bay's beach is ideal for a leisurely walk along the shoreline because it is dotted with soft pebbles and seashells. It's a great place for a quiet stroll because you can frequently discover intriguing marine life washed up.

- **Trekking**: Although there aren't any paths on the beach at Maho Bay, Virgin Islands National Park offers trekking options close by. From the Maho Bay area, you may reach the neighboring Francis Bay trail, which provides a picturesque path through the verdant greenery and along the shore.

What to anticipate:

- **Calm and Private Setting**: Maho Bay is typically less crowded than other well-known St. John beaches, providing a quiet and private setting. It's ideal for people looking for peace and a relaxed atmosphere.

- **Tranquil Waters**: Maho Bay's shallow, normally tranquil waters are perfect for swimming, snorkeling, and other aquatic activities. Because the bay is protected, there aren't many waves, making it a safe beach for families with little children.

- **Minimal Business Development**: Maho Bay has few business buildings nearby since it has been protected to preserve its natural charm. There are picnic tables, restrooms, and a small parking area, but no big resorts or eateries are located directly on the beach, preserving its unspoiled and tranquil feel.

Maho Bay

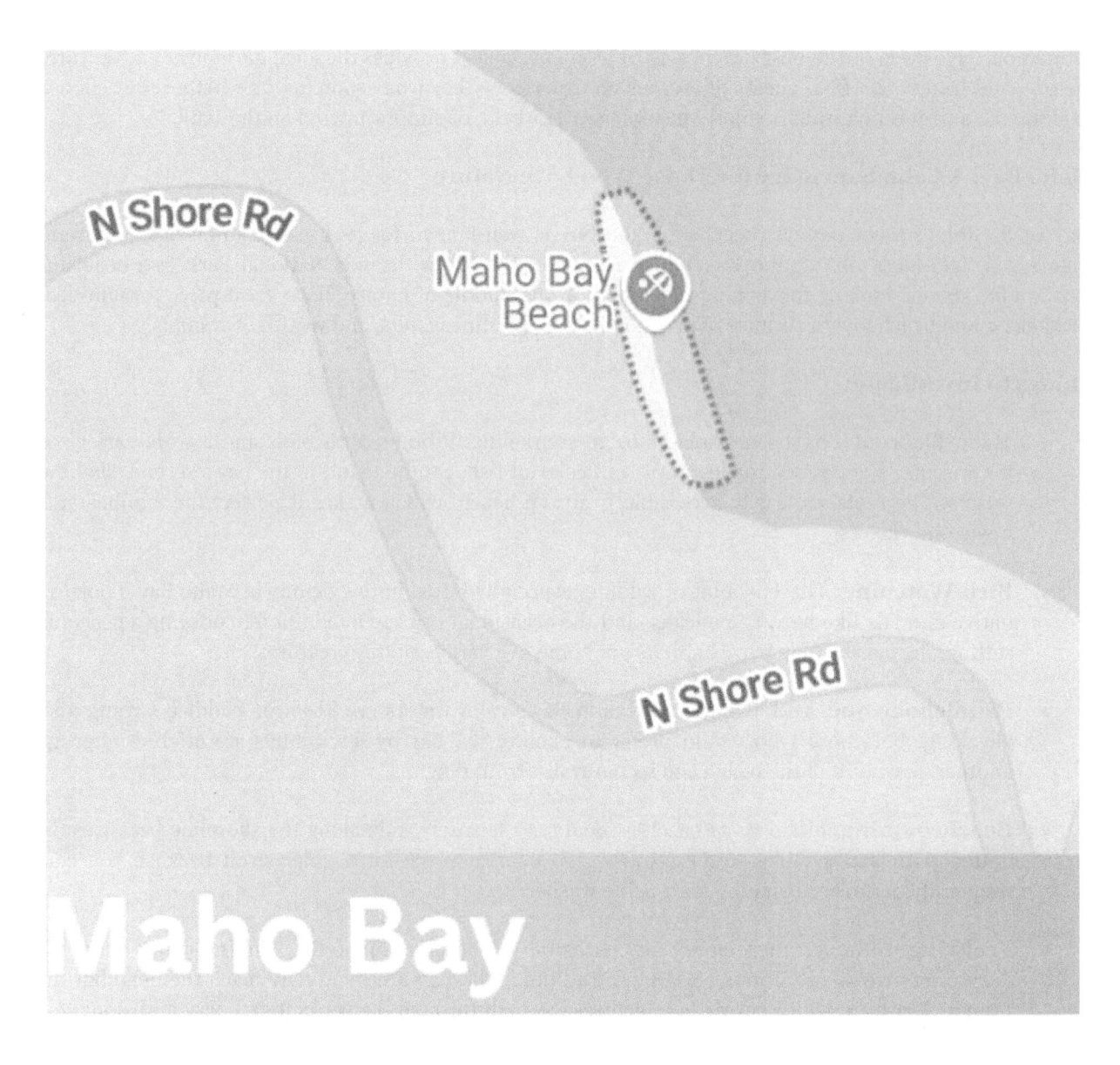

Scan the QR code

1. Open Camera: Launch your smartphone's camera app.
2. Position QR Code: Place the QR code within the camera's viewfinder.
3. Hold Steady: Keep the device steady for the camera to focus.
4. Wait for Scan: Wait for the code to be recognized.
5. Tap Notification: Follow the prompt to access the content.

- **Natural Shade**: Because of the trees that flank the beach, tourists may relax and take in the scenery without being exposed to the sun.

- **Tidal Changes**: Throughout the day, Maho Bay sees minor tidal changes. Checking tidal schedules is crucial, particularly if you intend to go snorkeling, as low tide makes some areas of the bay more accessible.

How to Get There:

- **By driving**: Cruz Bay is the starting point for a driving trip to Maho Bay. It takes about fifteen to twenty minutes to drive there. Take the Maho Bay turnoff off of Route 20, which takes you to a tiny parking lot close to the shore.

- **By Taxi**: Maho Bay may be reached immediately from Cruz Bay by taxi. Because there isn't as much public transportation in the area, it's best to plan a return trip with your driver in advance.

- **By Boat**: Maho Bay can be reached by dinghy for those who are on a boat. Although there isn't a dock or official mooring facilities, you can anchor off the bay and row to the beach.

Price:

- **Beach Access**: Since Maho Bay is a part of Virgin Islands National Park, which charges a $5 per person admission fee, there is no cost to enter.

- **Rentals**: The neighboring beach offers rentals for individuals who want to paddleboard, kayak, or snorkel. You should budget between $20 and $40 per hour for equipment.

- **Parking**: Maho Bay has a free parking lot, although there may not be as much room during peak hours. To guarantee a seat, it is advisable to arrive early.

Advice:

- **Arrive Early**: Try to visit Maho Bay early in the morning or late in the afternoon when there are fewer visitors for a more sedate experience.

- **Bring Your Water and Snacks**: Although there are picnic tables and restrooms, Maho Bay does not have any full-service restaurants, so it is advisable to pack your water and snacks. In order to stay hydrated under the sun, don't forget to bring enough water.

- **Rent Snorkel Gear:** To experience the marine life, rent or bring your snorkeling gear. Snorkeling is great here.

- **Watch the Tides:** Because some areas of the beach might not be reachable during high tide, be mindful of the bay's tidal fluctuations. Make appropriate plans for your visit.

- **Respect the Environment**: Keep in mind that Maho Bay is a protected location inside the Virgin Islands National Park. When snorkeling, be careful not to harm the coral reefs and don't disturb the species.

Accessibility: Because the beach is level and the parking lot is nearby, Maho Bay is somewhat accessible for those with mobility impairments. However, the rocky shoreline may make it difficult to reach the ocean, so visitors with limited mobility might wish to ask locals where the best access sites are.

Seasonal Considerations: December through April, when the weather is perfect for beach activities, is the greatest time of year to visit Maho Bay. Expect more rain during the off-season, but the beach is still lovely and less busy.

For those who enjoy the outdoors and want to relax in a serene, natural environment, Maho Bay is the ideal getaway. Maho Bay provides tourists with an ideal and peaceful experience, whether they choose to snorkel among the colorful coral reefs, relax beneath the trees, or just take in the beauty of St. John.

Chapter 5.Adventures in the Outdoors

Trails for Hiking

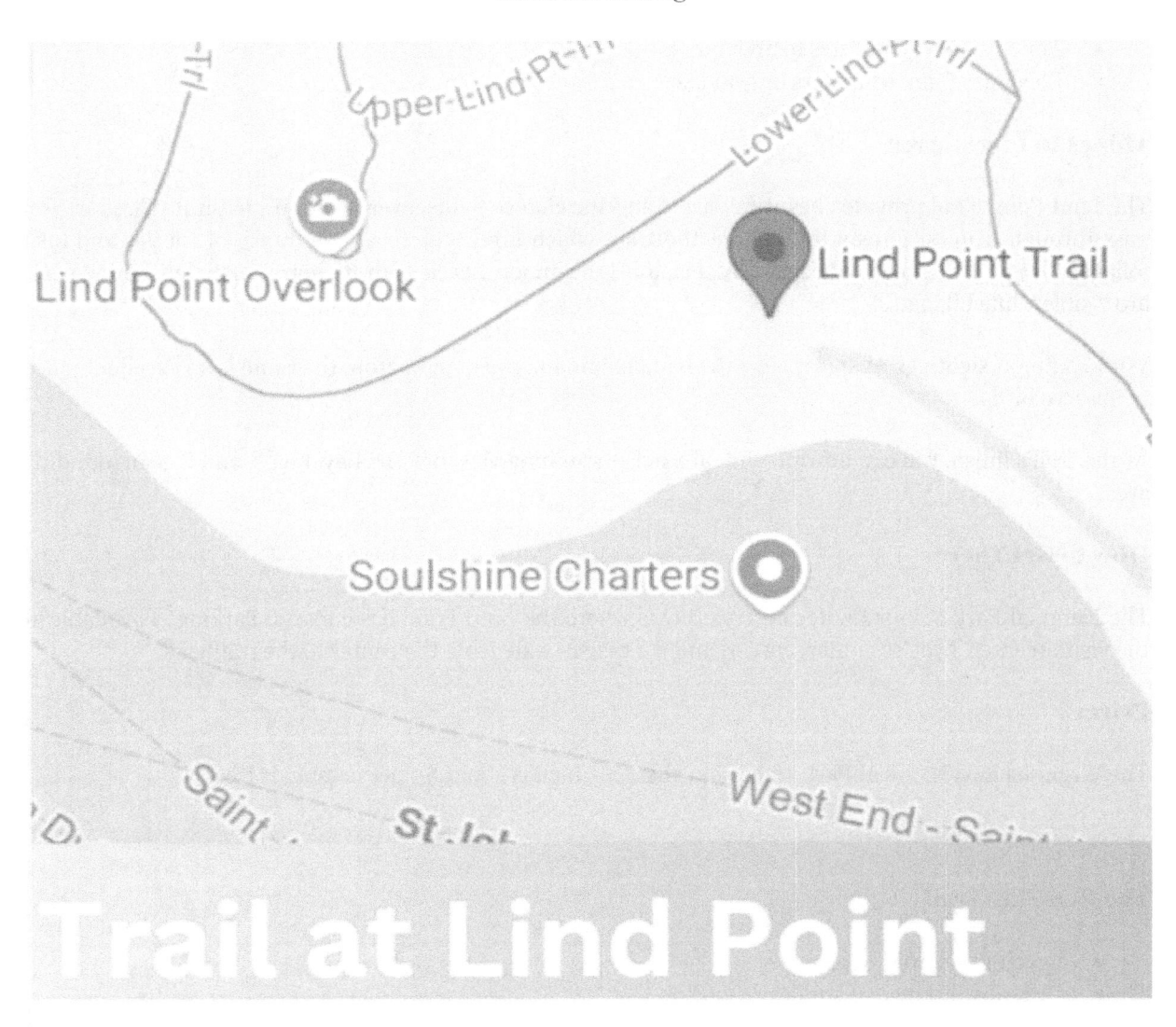

Trail at Lind Point

Scan the QR code

1. Open Camera: Launch your smartphone's camera app.
2. Position QR Code: Place the QR code within the camera's viewfinder.
3. Hold Steady: Keep the device steady for the camera to focus.
4. Wait for Scan: Wait for the code to be recognized.
5. Tap Notification: Follow the prompt to access the content.

Trail at Lind Point

- **Level**: Moderate to Easy
- Round-trip distance: 1.3 miles (2.1 km)
- Time frame: 45 minutes to an hour
- Elevation Gain: 91 meters or 300 feet

Things to Investigate:

The Lind Point Trail provides beautiful vistas and the chance to discover St. John's natural splendor. You pass through tropical forests throughout the trail, which are home to a wide range of species and lush foliage. Views of the nearby beaches, especially Honeymoon Beach with its immaculate, glistening seas, are visible while hiking.

With common sightings of species like the bananaquit and the green heron, the route is an excellent place to observe birds.

At the trail's finish, you can unwind and take in the stunning view of Cruz Bay, boats, and the surrounding area.

How to Get There:

The National Park Visitor Center in Cruz Bay is where the Lind Point Trail starts. Parking is available at the visitor center if you're coming by car, and it's easy to walk from the center to the trailhead.

Price:

The Virgin Islands National Park admission charge, which is about $5 per person, is free.

The Reef Bay Trail

- Level: From Mild to Intense
- One-way distance: 2.5 miles (4 km)
- Time frame: two to three hours
- Elevation Gain: 305 meters or 1,000 ft

Things to Investigate:

One of the most well-liked trails in St. John is the Reef Bay Trail, which passes through a variety of environments, such as lush rainforests, historic petroglyphs, and sugar plantation ruins. The trail leads to the stunning Reef Bay as it dips into the valley.

Historical relics that showcase St. John's colonial past can be found along the route, including the remnants of an old sugar mill and other plantation buildings.

Along with tropical birds, frogs, and butterflies, the Reef Bay Trail is home to a variety of animals, including the endangered St. John anole.

There is a picturesque bay at the trail's base that is ideal for swimming or unwinding before the climb back.

Additionally, there is the opportunity to view the well-known petroglyphs that the island's early residents cut into the rocks.

How to Get There:

Accessible by Route 10, just south of the junction with Route 20, the Reef Bay Trail starts at the trailhead close to the Reef Bay Sugar Mill Ruins. The trail is marked and simple to locate.

Since it's a difficult climb up, it's advised to take a shuttle or a guided hike to the trail's base. Many tourists choose to hike one way and have transportation back.

Price:

Free, although each person must pay $5 to enter the Virgin Islands National Park.

Depending on the tour operator, the price of a guided trek usually ranges from $50 to $100 per person.

The Brown Bay Trail

- Level: Moderate
- Round-trip distance: 1.5 miles (2.4 km)
- Time frame: one to one and a half hours
- Gain in elevation: 500 feet, or 152 meters

Things to Investigate:

Compared to the other well-traveled routes on St. John, the Brown Bay Trail provides a more isolated and tranquil hiking experience. Surrounded by dense woodland, the walk ends on a pristine beach where you may relish the peace.

You'll go through a variety of environments, including mangrove forests, and might see lizards, birds, and mongooses.

The actual Brown Bay is a charming, remote beach with quiet seas that is perfect for swimming or just lounging on the sand.

For hikers seeking a more secluded and uncrowded experience, the trail is an excellent choice.

How to Get There:

North Shore Road (Route 20) is where you'll find the trailhead for the Brown Bay Trail. It is close to the location of Cinnamon Bay Campground. It is advised to use a four-wheel-drive vehicle to approach the parking lot because the road leading to the trailhead is not paved.

Price:

Free, although each person must pay $5 to enter the Virgin Islands National Park.

The Francis Bay Trail

- Level: Simple
- One-way distance: 0.6 miles (1 km)
- Time frame: 30 to 45 minutes
- Elevation Gain: 30 meters or 100 feet

Things to Investigate:

The Francis Bay Trail is a short, family-friendly hike that follows a mangrove forest and passes through tropical greenery. The walk leads to Francis Bay, one of St. John's most stunning beaches, where you can take in views of the surrounding islands and the water.

For tourists seeking a brief hike with little exertion, this short track is ideal. It's a nice place for a swim or picnic because of the sandy beach and calm seas at the end of the hike.

Numerous native plants and animals, including fish, crabs, and tropical birds, can be seen along the route. For those who enjoy the outdoors, it's a serene and calm place.

How to Get There:

The Francis Bay parking lot, which is on Route 20, is close to the trailhead. The walk to the beach is quick and simple, and the trail is conveniently located near the parking lot.

Price:

Free, although each person must pay $5 to enter the Virgin Islands National Park.

These routes provide a range of experiences, from leisurely walks along the beach to strenuous hikes through the untamed landscape of St. John. Nature lovers and adventure seekers alike should not miss St. John's hiking paths, whether they provide breathtaking vistas, historical landmarks, or the opportunity to unwind on remote beaches.

Locations for Snorkeling and Diving

The Trunk Bay

Things to Investigate:

- With its vivid coral reefs and crystal-clear blue seas, Trunk Bay is one of St. John's most well-known snorkeling locations. Visitors can observe marine life, such as sea turtles, colorful fish, and occasionally rays, by going on the underwater snorkeling trail.

- With its immaculate white sand and serene waters, the beach itself is a popular destination for swimming and relaxing.

- Signs along the underwater trail direct snorkelers to a variety of sites of interest, such as coral formations and marine life.

What to anticipate:

- It's the perfect place for novice to intermediate snorkelers because of the clean waters and mild currents. While the deeper sections provide a more difficult experience, the shallow areas are ideal for beginners.

- The beach is convenient for day visitors because it provides amenities like showers, bathrooms, and rental equipment.

- Trunk Bay is one of the most popular beaches in the Virgin Islands National Park, so be prepared for crowds, particularly during the busiest travel seasons.

How to Get There:

- Cruz Bay is about ten minutes away from Trunk Bay, which is situated on North Shore Road (Route 20). There is a parking area at the beach, and driving there is simple.

- For a picturesque journey to Trunk Bay from Cruz Bay, use Route 20 east.

Price:

- $5 per person is the entrance charge to Virginia Islands National Park.

- **Equipment Rental**: You can hire snorkeling equipment for $15 to $20.

Advice:

- To avoid crowds and guarantee a decent place on the beach, get there early.

- There aren't many places to find shade on the beach, so bring a drink and sunscreen to stay hydrated.

- Because coral is delicate and easily destroyed, exercise caution when snorkeling and avoid touching it.

Bay of Cinnamon

Things to Investigate:

- With a wealth of marine life, including rays, sea turtles, and many fish species, Cinnamon Bay provides great snorkeling options. Beginners will love the shallow waters, while more experienced snorkelers may be able to enjoy more colorful coral reefs in the deeper sections.

- The bay offers a unique blend of history and scenic beauty, with a stunning beach around it and the opportunity to visit the neighboring ancient ruins of a sugar plantation.

What to anticipate:

- For those seeking a more tranquil snorkeling experience, Cinnamon Bay is the perfect spot because it is less crowded than some of St. John's more well-known beaches.

- With the possibility to rent snorkeling gear and spend a peaceful day on the ocean, the beach is still a terrific spot to unwind despite being less developed than other areas.

How to Get There:

- On the North Shore, Cinnamon Bay is situated immediately east of Trunk Bay on Route 20. There is plenty of on-site parking, and it is reachable by car.

Price:

- Since it is a component of the Virgin Islands National Park, admission is free; however, camping and lodging at Cinnamon Bay are subject to fees.

- **Equipment Rental**: It costs about $15 to $20 per day to rent snorkel equipment.

Advice:

- To capture the colorful aquatic life, bring a camera or an underwater case.

- There are some rocky spots in the bay's water, so wear water shoes.

- There may occasionally be strong currents in the area, so check the weather before you leave.

Bay of Maho

Things to Investigate:

- Some of the greatest snorkeling in St. John can be found at Maho Bay, a serene and charming beach. Numerous marine species can be found in the waters, such as colorful reef fish, rays, starfish, and green sea turtles.

- It's a great place for families and first-time snorkelers because of the shallow seas. The beach is frequently less busy than some of the other locations on the island, and the coral formations are in good condition.

What to anticipate:

- A relaxed atmosphere, fewer people, and an empty beach are to be expected. The tranquil waters are ideal for snorkeling and swimming at your leisure.

- Maho Bay is a great place for both novice and expert snorkelers because of its shallow entry and gentle slope.

- Additionally, there aren't many amenities at the beach, so pack your own drinks, food, and sunscreen.

How to Get There:

- On the North Shore, Maho Bay is situated along Route 20. There is a tiny parking lot next to the beach, and it is reachable by automobile. It's a quick stroll to the beach after parking.

Price:

- Free admission to the Virgin Islands National Park.
- **Equipment Rental**: A local store rents out snorkel gear, which usually costs between $15 and $20.

Advice:

- For the finest visibility and to minimize crowds, go early in the morning.
- To save the coral reefs, make sure you pack sunscreen that decomposes naturally.
- You might even be fortunate enough to see dolphins swimming right off the coast.

Cay Waterlemon

Things to Investigate:

- A quick kayak or boat ride from the shore will take you to Waterlemon Cay, a little island just off the coast of St. John. Rich coral reefs and a variety of marine life, such as schools of vibrant fish, rays, and sea turtles, can be found in the nearby waters.
- Because the Cay is a marine protected area, the waters are clear and provide great visibility for divers and snorkelers.
- The island's shallow waters make it simple to explore its underwater habitats, and it's a terrific place to unwind, swim, and snorkel for a few hours.

What to anticipate:

- Because Waterlemon Cay is very remote and only reachable by boat or kayak, expect a quiet and uncrowded experience.
- Clear, quiet waters make this a fantastic place for snorkeling because the coral reefs around the island are in good condition.
- Bring everything you'll need for a day out, such as water, snacks, and snorkeling equipment, as the island lacks facilities.

How to Get There:

To get to Waterlemon Cay, you must first park at the end of Route 20. From there, it's a quick and simple trek to the beach. From there, you can get to the cay via boat or by renting a kayak. As an alternative, you can schedule a boat tour with a guide.

Price:

- As a component of the Virgin Islands National Park, admission is free.
- Kayak Rental: Half-day rentals usually cost between $30 and $40.
- Guided Tours: Snorkeling tours with a guide can cost anything from $50 to $100 per person.

Advice:

- Since you will be rowing or kayaking to the cay, bring a dry bag for your things.

- The seas surrounding Waterlemon Cay can occasionally be a little stronger than other snorkeling locations, so pay attention to the tides and currents.

- Remember to use sunscreen that is safe for coral reefs and marine life.

From novices to experts, there is something for every kind of adventurer at these St. John diving and snorkeling locations. These locations in the Virgin Islands National Park provide remarkable experiences, whether you're searching for calm beaches, a plethora of marine life, or undiscovered undersea paths.

Chapter 6. Examining the National Park of the Virgin Islands

Must-See Locations

Cay Waterlemon

Things to Investigate:

- A tiny island called Waterlemon Cay is situated off the northeastern coast of St. John. It provides one of the greatest snorkeling experiences on the island and is a part of the Virgin Islands National Park.

- Schools of fish, rays, sea turtles, and colorful coral reefs abound in the nearby seas. Snorkelers of all skill levels will love the shallow waters.

- The island itself is deserted and encircled by immaculate beaches, providing tourists with a peaceful, natural setting.

What to anticipate:

- Anticipate a wealth of aquatic life and pristine seas. The Cay's snorkel trail offers great visibility and an immersive underwater experience.

- You can take in the natural beauty without being surrounded by a lot of people because the area is usually quiet and empty.

- Since the cay lacks amenities, guests should pack snacks, water, and sunscreen for a comfortable stay.

How to Get There:

- From the parking lot at the end of Route 20, it's a short stroll to Waterlemon Cay. From there, guests can get to the cay by boat or kayak. A guided snorkeling tour is another option for visiting the location.

Price:

- As a component of the Virgin Islands National Park, admission is free.

- Kayak Rental: A half-day rental costs about $30 to $40.

- Guided Tours: Usually cost between $50 and $100 per person.

Advice:

- To experience the neighborhood without crowds, arrive early.

- To save coral reefs and marine life, use sunscreen that is safe for reefs.

- If you plan to kayak to the cay, bring a dry bag for your valuables.

Bay of Salt Pond

Things to Investigate:

- On St. John's southeast coast sits the remote beach known as Salt Pond Bay. It is well-known for having calm seas that are perfect for swimming, snorkeling, and kayaking.

- Numerous fish species, sea turtles, and starfish are among the region's abundant marine life. There are hiking routes all around the bay, including one that leads to Ram Head, which provides breathtaking island-wide views.

- The bay is named for the surrounding Salt Pond, a salt flat that is accessible by foot.

What to anticipate:

- A calm, serene beach that is less crowded than other well-known beaches like Cinnamon Bay and Trunk Bay. It's perfect for a relaxing day of sunbathing or snorkeling.

- Although the waters are usually tranquil, tourists should be aware that strong currents can occasionally occur.

- Because there aren't many amenities at the beach, bring your water, sunscreen, and snacks.

How to Get There:

- From Cruz Bay, it's a short drive down Route 107 to Salt Pond Bay. It's a short stroll to the beach when you follow the directions to the parking lot.

Price:

- Free admission to the Virgin Islands National Park.

- Equipment Rental: Snorkel equipment may be rented in the area for $15 to $20.

Advice:

- Because the area is less developed, make sure you pack everything you'll need for the day.

- The trek to Ram Head, which provides some of the island's best views, is not to be missed.

- Before going snorkeling, check the tide charts because some places can get choppy.

Beach for Honeymoon

Things to Investigate:

- On the north side of St. John, Honeymoon Beach is a stunning and comparatively quiet beach with immaculate white sand and glistening waters ideal for swimming and snorkeling.

- With coral reefs and vibrant species, the beach's surrounding waters are serene and ideal for snorkeling. Sea turtles can frequently be seen swimming close to the beach, which is encircled by thick tropical flora.
- The Lind Point Trail leads to Honeymoon Beach, a well-liked location for hiking, kayaking, and paddleboarding.

What to anticipate:

- Anticipate a tranquil, romantic setting ideal for families and couples. Compared to some of the island's busier beaches, it is less crowded.
- There are opportunities to rent kayaks and paddleboards, but there aren't many amenities.
- The beach offers a tranquil location to take in St. John's natural splendor.

How to Get There:

- From Cruz Bay, you can drive or walk to Honeymoon Beach. To get to the beach from Cruz Bay, hike the picturesque 0.7-mile Lind Point Trail.
- As an alternative, you can paddle to the beach by renting a kayak or paddleboard from a local rental store.

Price:

- As a component of the Virgin Islands National Park, admission is free.
- **Equipment Rental:** Kayaks, paddleboards, and snorkeling equipment are available for $15 to $30 per hour.

Advice:

- To avoid crowds, especially during the busiest travel seasons, arrive early.
- There aren't many facilities, so bring your food and beverages.
- Be wary of the intense sun; wear a hat and lots of sunscreen for protection.

Ruins of the Annaberg Plantation

Things to Investigate:

- In the Virgin Islands National Park, the Annaberg Plantation Ruins are the remnants of a former sugar plantation. The plantation was an important part of the island's history and was in operation in the 18th century.

- The stone ruins, which include the remains of the factory, windmill, and other buildings, are open for exploration by tourists. The history of the plantation and the slave labor that drove the sugar business is also explained in the interpretative walk.

- The location provides breathtaking views of the nearby islands and the surrounding shoreline, making it a great place to take pictures.

What to anticipate:

- Anticipate a blend of natural beauty and history. The site is easily accessible from the parking area by a short, paved trail, and the ruins are in good condition.

- Despite its modest size, the plantation site provides a unique window into St. John's past, and the surrounding scenery is breathtaking.

- Bring your water and snacks because there aren't any significant amenities.

How to Get There:

- About ten minutes from Cruz Bay, on Route 20, are the Annaberg Plantation Ruins. There is parking at the site's entrance, and the plantation remains are only a short stroll away.

Price:

- As a component of the Virgin Islands National Park, admission is free.

Advice:

- For strolling on the uneven ground surrounding the ruins, wear strong shoes.

- Learn about the history of the plantation and the surrounding area by spending some time reading the informative inscriptions along the walk.

- There isn't much shade at the location, so bring a drink and sunscreen.

Conservation and Wildlife

St. John's Wildlife & Conservation

As a component of the Virgin Islands National Park, St. John is home to a wide variety of marine and terrestrial animals. Visitors may contribute significantly to the preservation of the island's natural beauty and ecological health, and conservation activities are essential to conserving this rich biodiversity.

St. John's wildlife

Marine Life:

- Because of the abundance of marine life in the surrounding waters, St. John is a well-liked snorkeling and diving destination.

- **Coral Reefs**: Home to species like brain coral, elkhorn coral, and stag-horn coral, St. John's coral reefs are among the healthiest in the Caribbean.

- **Fish Species**: Parrotfish, surgeonfish, and angelfish are among the many vibrant fish that snorkelers may come across.

- **Sea Turtles**: Green and hawksbill sea turtles are reported to inhabit the waters of St. John. Trunk Bay and Maho Bay are two locations where these turtles are frequently seen.

- **Sharks and Rays**: While diving or snorkeling, visitors may also see southern stingrays, nurse sharks, and perhaps even reef sharks.

- **Dolphins and Whales**: During their migratory seasons, bottlenose dolphins and humpback whales traverse the waters of St. John, offering nature enthusiasts a unique and thrilling experience.

Animals on Land:

- **Birds**: With a wide range of species, such as the endangered Virgin Islands parrot, frigatebirds, and brown pelicans, St. John is a birdwatcher's delight. The island is a fantastic place to go birdwatching all year round because it is also home to migratory species.

- **Invertebrates**: A variety of crab, spider, and insect species, including the endangered and protected St. John Rock Iguana, can be found on the island. Despite being endangered, these iguanas are frequently sighted in the island's arid woodlands.

- **Mammals**: Although there aren't many terrestrial mammals on the island, tourists might see small animals like mongoose, which were brought there years ago to help with pest control.

Conservation Activities

National Park of the Virgin Islands:

About 60% of St. John is protected by the Virgin Islands National Park, which was created in 1956. Numerous terrestrial and marine plant and animal species find refuge in the park, which protects the natural environment.

The park has contributed to the protection of numerous endangered species, like as sea turtles and native birds, making it an essential place for conservation.

Preservation of the Marine Environment:

- The Virgin Islands Coral Reef National Monument, a protected maritime region devoted to coral reef conservation and the preservation of endangered species like sea turtles and manatees, includes the waters around St. John.

- Regular assessments and repair projects are carried out by marine conservation organizations to shield coral reefs from harm brought on by pollution, overfishing, and climate change.

- Additionally, the National Park Service strives to inform tourists about the value of sustainable boating, diving, and snorkeling techniques.

Protection of Wildlife:

- Breeding initiatives and habitat restoration are part of the efforts to save the endangered Virgin Islands Parrot. Thanks to conservation efforts, the parrot, which was once on the verge of extinction, has witnessed a comeback in numbers.

- The National Park Service and conservation organizations aggressively safeguard another endangered species, the St. John Rock Iguana. Among the initiatives are habitat management and lowering the number of non-native species, such as mongooses, that prey on them.

Controlling Invasive Species:

The ecosystems of St. John are seriously threatened by non-native flora and invasive creatures like mongoose. In order to promote the growth of native plants and animals, conservation organizations are attempting to manage and eradicate invasive species.

In order to prevent invasive species from spreading across the natural landscape, efforts are also concentrated on habitat restoration.

How Tourists Can Help With Conservation

Be mindful of protected areas:

- It is recommended that visitors adhere to all park restrictions, stay on designated pathways, and refrain from upsetting any wildlife. Wildlife, particularly iguanas and sea turtles might have their natural behaviors disturbed and their health jeopardized when they are approached or fed.

Eco-Friendly Tasks:

- Divers and snorkelers are advised to use eco-friendly sunscreen and to behave in a "reef-safe" manner, avoiding contact with coral and marine life.

- Boating and kayaking should be done carefully to prevent harming delicate habitats, such as coral reefs and seagrass beds.

- Participate as a Volunteer and Help Local Conservation Groups:

- Volunteer opportunities and support for continuing conservation work are provided by several local organizations, such as Friends of Virgin Islands National Park. Participating in environmental education initiatives, wildlife monitoring, and beach clean-ups are ways that visitors can help.

Conscientious Travel:

- Supporting environmentally conscious establishments and lodgings that put sustainability first, such as those that emphasize waste reduction, energy conservation, and local sourcing, can help visitors preserve St. John's distinctive ecosystems.

The main draws of St. John and the secret to maintaining its natural beauty are its wildlife and conservation initiatives. Visitors may contribute to ensuring that this paradise is preserved and alive for future generations by engaging in conservation initiatives and practicing responsible tourism. Everyone may contribute to preserving the harmony between tourism and environmental conservation, whether it is by hiking trails, discovering marine life, or lending support to regional conservation organizations.

Chapter 7. Regional Food and Dining

Top Dining Establishments

At Caneel Bay, Zozo's

What to anticipate:

- Zozo's, a classy restaurant with breathtaking bay views, is situated in the center of Caneel Bay Resort. Zozo's, which is well-known for its sophisticated atmosphere, offers a Mediterranean and Caribbean-inspired menu that frequently uses locally produced fresh fish, meats, and vegetables. It is well known for its outdoor dining, which creates the ideal setting for taking in the sunset while dining.

How to Get There:

- The location of Zozo's is Caneel Bay, which is reachable by car or boat. You must enter the private Caneel Bay Resort property in order to reach the restaurant. Guests who are not staying at the resort need either rent a car or take a taxi to Caneel Bay, or they can take a boat from Cruz Bay.

Price:

- For an entrée, budget between $30 to $60 per person. Drinks and appetizers range in price from $12 to $15, with cocktails being the most expensive. Depending on the foods you select, the price may increase.

The Restaurant on the Terrace

What to anticipate:

- The Terrace Restaurant is a fine-dining establishment located on the grounds of The Westin St. John Resort Villas in the center of Cruz Bay. The restaurant has a classy yet laid-back ambiance with breathtaking views of the bay. Fresh seafood, steaks, and island-inspired sides are among its specialties, which include American cuisine with Caribbean influences. The Terrace is particularly well-known for its wide selection of wines, which go well with the cuisine.

How to Get There:

- The Terrace is situated in the heart of St. John, inside The Westin Resort, not far from Cruz Bay. From the major town, getting there by vehicle or taxi is simple. Another option is to walk to the resort after taking a boat to Cruz Bay.

Price:

- Depending on the cuisine, entrees might cost anywhere from $25 to $60. Seafood is typically more expensive. Desserts range from $8 to $12, while salads and appetizers cost between $10 and $15.

The Longboard

What to anticipate:

- The Longboard is a casual yet stylish beachside eatery that serves a variety of cuisines with an island flair and fresh fish. Fish tacos, grilled mahi-mahi, and jerk chicken are among the delicacies served at The Longboard, which is well-known for its tropical cocktails and laid-back atmosphere. It also offers a variety of refreshing drinks. With its outdoor eating area and Caribbean Sea breezes it's a terrific place for sunset dinners.

How to Get There:

- The Longboard is conveniently located at Cruz Bay and can be reached from anywhere on the island by car or taxi. The restaurant is located at the water's edge, so if you're staying close to Cruz Bay, you can easily walk there.

Price:

- The cost of each entrée should be between $15 and $35. Appetizers range in price from $8 to $15, while specialty cocktails cost from $10 to $12.

Seafood Market and Fish Trap Restaurant

What to anticipate:

- A neighborhood favorite, Fish Trap serves fresh, locally caught seafood and has a friendly atmosphere. Anticipate a range of foods, from simple grilled selections to Caribbean-spiced ones, such as grilled lobster, conch fritters, mahi-mahi, and shrimp. The restaurant, which is situated in Cruz Bay, offers both indoor and outdoor seating along with stunning harbor views. Additionally, it functions as a fish market where guests can buy fresh seafood to take home.

How to Get There:

- The ferry pier is only a short stroll from Fish Trap, which is conveniently situated in Cruz Bay. Walking from the town center or taking a quick taxi journey from anywhere on the island will get you to the restaurant with ease.

Price:

- Fresh fish is the main focus of entrees, which normally cost between $20 and $45. The cost of appetizers, such as shrimp cocktails and conch fritters, ranges from $8 to $12. Depending on the catch of the day, you can also buy fresh fish at the seafood market for a variety of costs.

Specialties from the Island

Fritters with Conch

Components:

- Conch, a kind of shellfish native to the Caribbean, is the primary ingredient in conch fritters. Chopped conch flesh, flour, cornmeal, eggs, milk, onion, bell pepper, garlic, and seasonings (such as salt, pepper, and thyme) are combined to make the fritters. After that, the mixture is deep-fried till crispy and golden. The fritters are frequently served with a tartar sauce hot remoulade, or another acidic dipping sauce.

Where to Purchase Them:

- In the Virgin Islands, conch fritters are a common dish, particularly at small cafes and seafood restaurants. The Longboard at Cruz Bay and Fish Trap Restaurant & Seafood Market are two excellent spots in St. John to have conch fritters.

Price:

An appetizer of conch fritters usually costs $8 to $12. The location and portion size may have an impact on prices.

Mahi-Mahi

Components:

The solid, white mahi-mahi, sometimes referred to as dolphin fish, is frequently seen in the warm waters surrounding the Virgin Islands. It is usually served with tropical fruits or a tasty sauce, like mango salsa or garlic-butter sauce, and is frequently grilled, fried, or baked. Side dishes that go well with it include fries, rice, and veggies.

Where to Purchase Them:

The majority of St. John's seafood restaurants serve mahi-mahi. The Terrace Restaurant, The Lime Inn, and Zozo's in Caneel Bay are a few suggested locations.

Price:

A mahi-mahi entrée should cost between $25 and $40, depending on the restaurant's prices and the preparation process. Mahi-mahi may be served as a special at some restaurants; the price may vary.

Roti

Components:

Indian and Caribbean cuisines are the origins of the roti, a sort of flatbread. The dough is often fried on a griddle and is composed of flour, water, and salt. Roti is frequently served with curried meats, like beef, goat, or chicken, and occasionally with vegetables. The most popular roti varieties in St. John are stuffed with curried meat, chicken, or veggies to make a tasty, filling supper.

Where to Purchase Them:

Around St. John, roti is served at food stands and Caribbean-style eateries. Sheen's Caribbean Flavors, which specializes in real Caribbean food, is among the greatest spots to eat roti. For a variation on classic roti dishes, visit Café Roma as well.

Price:

Depending on the filling and portion sizes served at the restaurant, a roti meal usually costs between $10 and $20.

Cakes, Johnny

Components:

In the Caribbean, fried cornmeal dough cakes, or "johnny cakes," are a common side dish. Cornmeal, sugar, salt, baking powder, and water (sometimes coconut milk for taste) are the ingredients used to make the dough. After that, they are fried until they turn golden brown. Johnny cakes are frequently served as an accompaniment to savory foods like curries or fried fish, or with butter or honey.

Where to Purchase Them:

Johnny cakes can be found all across St. John and the Virgin Islands, particularly at Caribbean restaurants and neighborhood diners. They can be found at Morgan's Mango, Rhum Room, or The Lime Inn.

Price:

Depending on whether they are served as an accompaniment or with other foods, Johnny cakes usually cost between $3 and $8. They might be served as part of a larger dinner at some places.

Chapter 8. Experiences with Culture

Events and Festivals

Festival of St. John (July 4th)

When:

- Every year, the St. John Festival—also called the July 4th Festival—occurs from the end of June to the beginning of July, with July 4th serving as the focal point of the celebrations.

Where:

- Parades, concerts, and street parties are among the festivities that take place throughout the island during the festival, which is held in Cruz Bay, St. John.

What to anticipate:

- With musicians, dancers, and local groups participating in colorful parades, expect a lively celebration of the area's culture. Additionally, there are food vendors serving regional Caribbean delicacies, musical acts, and firework displays. The festival is a wonderful opportunity to take in St. John's vibrant atmosphere and sense of community while also showcasing local arts and crafts.

How to Get There:

- Cruz Bay, which is reachable by ferry from St. Thomas, is the focal point of the celebration. The majority of events at Cruz Bay may be reached by foot. To get to the island during the celebrations, you can also rent a car or use a cab.

Price:

- Although some events, like special performances or events, may need an admission fee, the festival itself is free to attend. Local sellers' food and beverages usually cost between $5 and $20.

Carnival in the Virgin Islands

When:

- Every year, though the exact dates may change, the Virgin Islands Carnival takes place in April or May. The major parade usually takes place during the first week of May, and the carnival lasts for many weeks.

Where:

- Although the carnival is held in St. Thomas, participants come from all across the Virgin Islands, including St. John.

What to anticipate:

- With parades, live music, dances, and a spectacular display of Caribbean culture, the Virgin Islands Carnival is a significant occasion. Large, vibrant floats, performers in costume, and traditional Caribbean music—such as steel pan bands, calypso, and reggae—are all to be expected. In addition, there are contests, food vendors serving Caribbean specialties, and a joyous mood all around. Attending the event is a fantastic chance to learn about the Virgin Islands' dynamic culture.

How to Get There:

- It takes roughly fifteen minutes to travel by ferry from St. John to St. Thomas. Once in St. Thomas, the major carnival activities are held in and around Charlotte Amalie, where you may travel to the festivities by taxi or public transit.

Price:

- The majority of carnival activities, including parades and open entertainment, are free. However, tickets, which usually cost between $20 and $50, may be necessary for certain private events or parties.

The St. John Arts Festival

When:

- Usually taking place over many days in January, the St. John Arts Festival features performances, workshops, and exhibitions.

Where:

- The festival is held in a number of locations throughout Cruz Bay, such as neighborhood eateries, galleries, and public areas. Events might potentially spread to neighboring places like Coral Bay.

What to anticipate:

- The event honors St. John's inventiveness and rich cultural legacy. Expect musical music, artisan fairs, art exhibits, and local artists' performances. Additionally, there are engaging seminars where participants can pick up regional skills like ceramics or basketry. The festival offers an excellent opportunity to become fully immersed in the local culture and discover St. John's cultural community.

How to Get There:

- Cruz Bay, which is reachable by ferry from St. Thomas, is the venue for the event. Events are usually within walking distance of Cruz Bay, though those who want to see more of the island can hire a car or take a cab.

Price:

- Attendance at many events, including performances and exhibitions, is free. However, there can be a minor price for some seminars or special events, usually between $10 and $30.

The St. John Film Festival

When:

- Every year, usually over a weekend, the St. John Film Festival takes place in June. The festival presents a variety of films, including documentaries and independent features.

Where:

- The festival is held in Cruz Bay at locations like the neighborhood theater or open-air movie theaters. Some screenings in other parts of St. John are also included.

What to anticipate:

- Independent films, documentaries, and short films that examine a range of subjects, such as the history, culture, and ecology of the Virgin Islands, are the main emphasis of the St. John Film Festival. The festival also includes discussions, Q&A sessions, and filmmaker meet-and-greets. A rare chance to experience St. John's more artistic and cultural side is provided by the event.

How to Get There:

- Cruz Bay, which is conveniently reachable by ferry from St. Thomas, is the site of the festival. Although taxis or rental automobiles can be employed for further distances or to further explore the island, venues are accessible on foot from the Cruz Bay ferry station.

Price:

- The average price of a ticket to see a movie is between $10 and $20. There may be extra fees for special events like workshops or VIP experiences.

Regional Crafts and Art

Crafts & Local Art on St. John

The island's rich history, culture, and scenic beauty are all reflected in St. John's thriving arts and crafts industry. A wide range of handcrafted items, including jewelry, textiles, ceramics, and paintings, are available for visitors to purchase as ideal mementos or souvenirs. A closer look at the local craft and art scene is provided here:

What to anticipate:

- **Handmade Jewelry**: Using locally found materials like coral, shells, and semi-precious stones, St. John's artists craft gorgeous items. These distinctive designs, which create one-of-a-kind works that perfectly encapsulate the spirit of the island, are offered for sale in galleries and at neighborhood markets.

- **Paintings and Photographs:** St. John's natural scenery, colorful sunsets, and beach sceneries serve as inspiration for many local artists. You can anticipate seeing a variety of artwork, such as prints from photographs, watercolors, and oil paintings. The island's tranquil waters, fauna, and tropical beauty are frequently portrayed in these works.

- **Woodworking & Carvings**: Using hardwoods that are frequently acquired locally, St. John's woodworkers create elaborate sculptures and figures. Art galleries and stores carry wooden objects such as carved figures, cutting boards, and bowls.

- **Pottery and Ceramics**: Beautiful pottery, ranging from decorative vases to useful plates and mugs, is created by local ceramic craftsmen. These pieces are a wonderful way to bring a bit of the island into your house and are frequently inspired by the island's natural environment.

- **Textiles & Clothes**: St. John's artisans are known for their handwoven baskets, hand-dyed textiles, and island-inspired apparel. These products frequently have vivid, striking designs that draw inspiration from the Caribbean landscape.

- **Handmade Soap and Candles**: Using natural ingredients like coconut, aloe, and locally cultivated herbs and flowers, local artists make soaps and candles with tropical fragrances. These handcrafted items add a soothing island element to your everyday routine.

Where to Look for Crafts and Art in Your Area:

Cruz Bay's Mongoose Junction is a well-known retail district with a number of art galleries and craft stores selling a variety of locally produced jewelry, artwork, and handicrafts.

- **The Marketplace (Cruz Bay):** The Marketplace features art galleries with regional paintings, photographs, and other one-of-a-kind items in addition to stores selling apparel and trinkets.

- **Coral Bay:** In addition to having tiny local stores that sell homemade items like jewelry, pottery, and textiles, Coral Bay is less developed than Cruz Bay.

- **Farmers Markets and Local Festivals**: You can buy handcrafted things straight from the artists by going to St. John's farmers markets or art festivals. Local artists' creations are on display during events such as the St. John Arts Festival, where vendors sell anything from handmade baskets to jewelry.

What to anticipate while making a purchase:

- Smaller products like jewelry or handcrafted soaps may cost a few dollars, while larger works like original paintings or sculptures may cost several hundred dollars. The time and materials used to create each piece are frequently reflected in the price.

- Buying many of the products on the island supports the community and local artisans because they are made with sustainable methods.

Ways to Encourage Regional Crafts and Art:

- To guarantee that the artists get a fair portion of the sales, purchase directly from nearby galleries or artists.

- To meet the artists and discover more about the creative process, think about going to art festivals and exhibitions.

- Don't be afraid to ask if you're seeking something specific; many artists and galleries also create custom creations.

St. John's art sector offers a variety of options that capture the essence and charm of the island, whether you're searching for something useful, like pottery, or a one-of-a-kind piece of art to decorate your house. Encouraging regional craftspeople guarantees the survival of the island's cultural legacy.

Chapter 9. Insider Advice

The Best Times to Go

The Greatest Times to Go to St. John

Although St. John is a stunning place to visit all year round, the time of year you go can have a big impact on how much fun you have. Whether you value less crowds, better weather, or cheaper costs, the ideal time to come will depend on your priorities. The benefits and drawbacks of traveling at different times of year are broken down here:

Season of Peak Interest (December to April)

Advantages:

The best weather occurs during this time of year when balmy temperatures often range from 75°F to 85°F (24°C to 29°C). It's ideal for outdoor pursuits like hiking, snorkeling, and beach lounging because it's usually sunny, humid, and rainy.

- **Festivities & Events**: The Virgin Islands Carnival, St. John Festival, and other cultural events are taking place now if you want to experience local festivities.

- **Full Range of Services**: During this time, the majority of resorts, eateries, and excursions are open and running, guaranteeing a variety of dining and entertainment options.

Cons:

- **Expensive**: Because of the surge in tourists, airfare and lodging costs are at their highest points. In addition to being more costly, popular restaurants and resorts may need reservations made far in advance.

- **Overcrowded Beaches and Trails**: During holidays like Christmas and New Year's, the island can get crowded. Beaches and popular sights like Trunk Bay can get congested.

- **Limited Availability**: Because of the high demand, it can be more difficult to acquire last-minute reservations or discounts, and some events might sell out in advance.

Season of the Shoulders (May to June, November)

Advantages:

- **Excellent Weather**: With temperatures between 75°F and 85°F (24°C and 29°C), the weather is still excellent. Even while rain showers could occur occasionally, they are usually short and won't disrupt your plans.

- **Reduced Costs**: Flight and hotel rates are typically less expensive than at the busiest times of the year, giving budget-conscious tourists additional options.

- **Less Crowded**: There are fewer people on the island, which makes for a calmer and more comfortable stay. On restaurants, hiking trails, and beaches, you'll have more room.

- **Good for Outdoor Activities**: Without the heavy crowds of peak season, this is a great time to experience St. John's outdoor activities, such as hiking and snorkeling.

Cons:

- **Hurricane Season Begins (June):** Although the official hurricane season lasts from June to November, May and early June are less dangerous. But in late June and into the fall, there is a greater chance of a hurricane or tropical storm.

- **Fewer Events**: Those hoping for big celebrations may be let down because, although there are still a few local events and festivals at this time, there aren't as many going on as there are during the busiest season.

From July to October, the off-season

Advantages:

- **Lowest Prices**: Flights, lodging, and tours are most affordable during the off-season. The island's tranquil setting makes it an affordable choice, and hotels and resorts frequently provide substantial discounts.

- **Fewer Crowds**: You'll have the island mostly to yourself because many tourists are avoiding it because of the heat and possible storms. For those looking for solitude or calm on the beach or when hiking, this is the ideal time of year.

- **Excellent for a Calm Getaway**: The off-season offers a much-needed respite from the tourist horde if you're hoping to get away from the crowds and relax without interruptions.

Cons:

- The island experiences hot and muggy weather, with some days reaching as high as 95°F (35°C), even if the temperature is still moderate and frequently rises beyond 85°F (29°C). If you're not acclimated to the heat, this may make outdoor activities more uncomfortable.

- **Increased Risk of Rain and Hurricanes**: Since the summer months fall during the height of hurricane season, there is an increased chance of storms and heavy rain. Hurricanes rarely strike St. John directly, but it's important to consider while making travel plans.

- **Restricted Services**: During the off-season, there are fewer events and activities available, and some resorts, eateries, and tours may close or only be open for a limited time.

December through April (peak season) is the best time for ideal weather and events.

- **Advantages**: Perfect weather, exciting events, and fully functional services
- **Cons**: Expensive, congested beaches, scarce supply

May through June and November (shoulder season) are the best times to get deals and avoid crowds.

- **Advantages**: Better weather, lower costs, and fewer visitors
- **Cons**: Fewer events and the beginning of storm season

The best time to travel on a budget and in peace is from July to October (off-season).

- **Advantages**: Best rates, peaceful setting
- **Cons**: Limited services, increased likelihood of rain and storms, and hot weather

The ideal time to visit St. John ultimately comes down to personal taste. It is best to visit during the busiest time of year if you want to take advantage of the great weather and exciting events. The shoulder and off-seasons provide a more tranquil experience with some discounts if you're more frugal and like calmer settings.

Advice for Eco-Friendly Travel

Tips for Eco-Friendly Travel to St. John

- Protecting the island's fragile ecosystem is crucial since St. John is a paradise renowned for its unspoiled scenery and abundant biodiversity. By traveling sustainably, you, as a visitor, may contribute to the preservation of the island's natural beauty. The following advice can help you have a positive island vacation while reducing your environmental impact:

Honor wildlife and the environment.

- When hiking, stay on established pathways to preserve native plants and their ecosystems.
- Steer clear of upsetting wildlife by not feeding them or approaching them too closely.
- Avoid touching coral reefs or marine creatures while snorkeling as this might damage fragile ecosystems.
- Beaches and parks should not have shells, sand, or plants removed.

Opt for Eco-Friendly Transportation

- To cut down on carbon emissions, walk or hire a bicycle for quick excursions around the island.
- When possible, take public transit, such as the St. John buses, to reduce your carbon footprint.

- To cut emissions, choose a hybrid or fuel-efficient car if you have to rent one.

- Think about going on a boat excursion run by businesses that adhere to sustainability standards, including not anchoring close to coral reefs.

Remain in Eco-Friendly Lodging

- Seek out environmentally conscious hotels and resorts that use sustainable practices, like trash reduction, water conservation, and energy conservation.

- Select lodgings that are dedicated to lessening their impact on the environment, such as those with green certification or solar power.

- Engage in initiatives that support sustainability, such as reusing towels and linens to cut down on laundry electricity usage.

Cut Down on Plastic Use

- To cut down on single-use plastic waste, always carry a reusable water bottle.

- Bring your own environmentally friendly straws, cutlery, or glasses instead of plastic ones, such as bamboo or stainless steel.

- Make use of reusable toiletry bottles and choose goods with recyclable or minimum packaging.

Encourage Sustainable and Local Businesses

- Purchase locally produced food, souvenirs, and crafts to help the St. John's community and lessen the negative effects of imports on the environment.

- Eat at restaurants that sell sustainable, locally based cuisine; stay away from eateries that utilize a lot of packaging or foods that aren't from the area.

- Choose eco-friendly tour companies and events that put an emphasis on sustainable tourism and responsible tourism, such as reducing trash and encouraging environmental education.

Use waste management techniques.

- If there isn't a bin accessible, carry your rubbish with you to dispose of later. Always dispose of trash appropriately.

- Take part in community events that preserve St. John's environment, such as beach clean-ups.

- Littering on beaches, hiking trails, and public areas should be avoided since it may quickly damage ecosystems and wildlife.

Save marine life and coral reefs.

- To shield coral reefs from dangerous chemicals that could harm marine life, use sunscreen that is safe for reefs.

- Avoid anchoring yachts on coral reefs as this can harm the fragile environment for a long time.

- Support local companies or groups that work to save coral reefs and marine life as a way to get involved in marine conservation initiatives.

Conserve Energy and Water

- Pay attention to how much water you use. Because a large portion of St. John's water supply comes from rainwater collecting, try to cut back on showers and water use.

- To help save energy, turn off lights and appliances when not in use.

- Steer clear of single-use or throwaway items that add to garbage whether you're at a beach or nature park.

- Find Out About Local Conservation Initiatives

- Spend some time learning about the island's conservation initiatives and lending your support to projects that will help maintain its natural beauty. To learn more about eco-friendly travel strategies in the Virgin Islands, visit the visitor center of the park.

- Take part in educational events or nature hikes that teach about the island's ecosystems, wildlife, and plants, as well as how to preserve them.

- By adhering to these environmentally responsible travel guidelines, you contribute to preserving St. John as a stunning and sustainable vacation spot for years to come. Even the smallest of efforts helps to protect the island's priceless animals and ecology.

Chapter 10. Useful Information

Itineraries

Three-Day Schedule for St. John

Day 1: Beach Day and Arrival

Morning:

- Reach St. John (via airline, automobile, or ferry).
- Check into your lodging (either an eco-friendly alternative or a luxury resort).
- One of the island's most well-known beaches, Trunk Bay, is a great place to unwind and rest.

In the afternoon

- Discover Cinnamon Bay, another stunning beach renowned for its tranquil setting.
- Savor a laid-back lunch at Cinnamon Bay Café, which serves regional and fresh fare.

Evening:

- At Honeymoon Beach, take in the sunset.
- Dinner at Zozo's at Caneel Bay, which provides a classy dining experience while taking in breathtaking views.

Day 2: Hiking and National Park Exploration

Morning:

- For a gentle and picturesque journey that offers views of the coastline and verdant surroundings, begin with the Lind Point Trail.
- For a more strenuous journey that passes historic sugar mills and prehistoric petroglyphs, head to Reef Bay Trail.

In the afternoon

- Lunch at The Longboard, a neighborhood restaurant serving delectable tropical fare.
- Discover the history of the island by visiting the Annaberg Plantation Ruins.
- Go snorkeling with amazing marine life at Waterlemon Cay by boat.

Evening:

- Enjoy Caribbean-inspired cuisine at The Terrace Restaurant while having a laid-back supper.
- Enjoy a laid-back evening at the bar at Gallows Point Resort to cap off the day.

Day 3: Cultural, artistic, and adventurous

Morning:

- Rent a kayak or paddleboard in Maho Bay to start the day.
- After that, go snorkeling and explore the underwater world at Salt Pond Bay.

In the afternoon

- Fish Trap Restaurant & Seafood Market for lunch.
- Visit the Virgin Islands National Park Visitor Center in the afternoon to find out more about the park's conservation initiatives.
- Investigate Cruz Bay's local art galleries and stores.

Evening:

- Savor a meal at The Beach Bar at Maho Bay beside the beach.
- Take a walk on the beach and have a nightcap at one of the neighborhood bars to cap off the trip.

7-Day St. John Itinerary

Day 1: Arrival and leisure at the beach

Morning:

- When you get to St. John, check into the hotel or resort of your choice.

In the afternoon

- Spend the afternoon on one of the world's most stunning beaches by traveling to Trunk Bay.

Evening:

- Dinner at Caneel Bay's Zozo's, a great place to eat well by the water.

Day 2: Cultural Exploration and Island Tour

Morning:

- Take a guided tour of the Annaberg Plantation Ruins to start the day.

- Discover the history and shopping of Cruz Bay.

In the afternoon

- Stop by The Longboard for lunch.

- Take a trip along the Reef Bay Trail to see historical landmarks, such as petroglyphs.

- Explore Cruz Bay's local marketplaces and shops during the afternoon.

Evening:

- After supper at The Terrace Restaurant, spend the evening relaxing in the bar of Gallows Point Resort.

Day 3: Exploration of National Parks

Morning:

- For breathtaking views of the island's natural beauty and shoreline, hike the Lind Point Trail.

In the afternoon

- Go swimming or snorkeling in Salt Pond Bay.

- Cinnamon Bay Café for lunch.

- Enjoy a leisurely dip in Cinnamon Bay.

Evening:

- Maho Bay's The Beach Bar for dinner.

- Savor a tranquil evening by the shore.

Day 4: Adventures in Snorkeling and Diving

Morning:

- At Waterlemon Cay, which is home to colorful coral reefs and a variety of marine life, spend the morning snorkeling.

In the afternoon

- Fish Trap Restaurant & Seafood Market for lunch.

- To see deeper underwater scenery, go on a diving cruise in Cinnamon Bay.

Evening:

- A laid-back evening at Honeymoon Beach while the sun was setting.
- Dinner at the restaurant at Gallows Point Resort.

Day 5: An Exciting Adventure Day

Morning:

- Explore Maho Bay and its gorgeous waters by renting a kayak or paddleboard.
- To go snorkeling again, consider kayaking or paddleboarding to Waterlemon Cay.

In the afternoon

- Visit Cruz Bay's The Terrace Restaurant for lunch.
- For a beautiful stroll and discovery, head to the Hiking Brown Bay Trail.

Evening:

- Zozo's in Caneel Bay offers fine dining and sunset views for dinner.

Day 6: Shopping and Local Arts

Morning:

- Explore neighborhood art galleries in Cruz Bay that specialize in distinctive crafts and Caribbean art.

In the afternoon

- The Longboard for lunch.
- Shop for jewelry, souvenirs, and regional crafts during the day.
- For information on local animals and conservation initiatives, visit the Visitor Center at Virgin Islands National Park.

Evening:

- Savor dinner at The Beach Bar while admiring the vibrant tropical ambiance.

Day 7: Unwind and Relax

Morning:

- Swim, sunbathe, and unwind in Trunk Bay in the morning.

In the afternoon

- Savor lunch at Cinnamon Bay Café or another coastal café.
- Take it easy at Salt Pond Bay or Maho Bay for the remainder of the afternoon.

Evening:

- Enjoy a sunset meal at Fish Trap Restaurant & Seafood Market to round off your journey.
- To think back on the wonderful island memories, take one more stroll down the shore.

These itineraries provide a well-balanced combination of leisure, exploration, and cultural encounters, enabling you to fully appreciate St. John's natural beauty while also learning about its lesser-known attractions.

Essentials for Traveling

ID and passport

- Americans visiting St. John must have a valid passport or other official identification.
- Outside the United States. Visa requirements should be checked in advance by citizens.

Insurance for Travel

- Strongly advised for trip protection, including trip cancellation and medical coverage.

Money

- The official currency is the US dollar (USD).
- Although most places take credit cards, it's still a good idea to have cash on hand for minor transactions.

Safety and Health

- Bring along any prescription drugs you may need.
- Basics like bandages, disinfectants, and painkillers are helpful in a travel first-aid pack.
- Think about getting travel health insurance.

Power and Adapters

- St. John has the same 110V voltage as the US mainland.
- For Type A and Type B U.S. plugs, no adapters are required.

- Getting Ready for the Weather

- Because of St. John's tropical environment, bring breezy, light clothing for hot days and a light jacket for chilly nights.

- Sunscreen, sunglasses, and a hat are necessities.

- The island occasionally experiences rain showers, so pack waterproof gear like a poncho or rain jacket.

Beach Equipment

- Water shoes, snorkeling equipment, and swimwear for beach and coral reef exploration.

- A mat or beach towel to relax on.

- A water-resistant bag or case to protect valuables and devices.

Shoes

- Comfortable walking shoes for island exploration and hiking paths.

- For beach days, wear flip-flops or sandals.

Water and Snacks

- To stay hydrated, especially when trekking, use a reusable water container.

- Bring small snacks (nuts, energy bars, etc.) for hikes or day excursions.

Electronics & Camera

- A phone case or waterproof camera to record aquatic and beach scenes.
- Your electrical devices can be charged on the go.
- If you're coming from overseas, don't forget to bring adapters.

Essentials of Transportation

- A current driver's license if you're renting a scooter or automobile.

- Navigating the island with maps or applications (download offline maps for distant places).

- Tickets for the ferry (if traveling from St. Thomas or other neighboring islands).

Backpack or Daypack

- A compact bag to hold necessities for everyday excursions, such as water, sunscreen, and snacks.

Sustainable Travel Products

- To reduce trash, use reusable containers, bags, and utensils.

- Sunscreen that decomposes naturally to safeguard coral reefs and the environment.

- WiFi or a local SIM card

- For Wi-Fi or data connectivity, think about purchasing a local SIM card.

- Free Wi-Fi is available at many cafes, restaurants, and resorts, however, it can be useful to have a portable hotspot.

- Emergency Numbers and Local Information

- Maintain a contact list for emergencies, which should include the local emergency number (911).

- The Myrah Keating Smith Community Health Center is the island's medical facility.

- Make sure you have the numbers for your guides, transportation, and lodging.

These travel necessities, which include everything from safety to beach activities and adventure excursions, will guarantee a hassle-free and delightful trip to St. John.

Etiquette and Safety

Safety Advice

Safety in general

- St. John is a somewhat secure place to visit, but as with any tourist location, you should exercise caution, particularly in less crowded regions.

- Avoid going for a nighttime stroll by yourself, especially on beaches or in isolated places.

- When not in use, keep your valuables—such as your passport, cash, and electronics—safe and hidden.

Water and Beach Safety

- Be aware of the water's conditions and only swim in locations that have been designated for that purpose.

- Observe any signs warning of jellyfish, strong currents, and other possible dangers.

- When diving and snorkeling, exercise caution and, for more difficult locations, think about hiring a guide.

Safety of Hiking

- To prevent getting lost when touring St. John's trails, stick to the designated routes. Use a trail app or bring a map.

- For longer hikes, especially, bring lots of water and wear sturdy shoes.

- Be mindful of local fauna, such as snakes, scorpions, and other animals, and maintain a respectful distance.

Numbers for Emergencies

- 911 for emergency services

- The Myrah Keating Smith Community Health Center at Cruz Bay is the primary medical facility on the island.

Awareness of Wildlife

- Honor the island's fauna, especially the coral reefs and sea turtles, which are threatened.

- Avoid feeding animals and do not disturb wildlife since this can interfere with their normal behaviors.

etiquette

- Observe local customs and traditions.

- Because St. John is a small, tight-knit town, it's critical to show consideration for the customs and culture of the area.

- Be courteous and receptive when interacting with residents. Although people on the island are typically amiable, good relationships are fostered by respecting the native way of life.

Tipping

Like the U.S. mainland, tipping is common in St. John:

- 15% to 20% of the total cost goes to restaurants (more for great service).

- Housekeeping staff at the hotel: $1–2 per day.

- For day outings or snorkeling excursions, tour guides cost $10–20 per person.

- 10–15% of the fare goes to the taxi drivers.

Environmental Responsibilities

- Clean up after oneself on hiking trails and beaches to practice "leave no trace."

- Protect marine life, especially coral reefs, which are extremely susceptible to chemicals, by using biodegradable sunscreen.

- Recycle and properly dispose of waste in the appropriate bins.

Dress and Conduct

- Although the island is relaxed and informal, modest clothing is advised when in public places, especially in villages or close to places of worship.

- Swimsuits and other beachwear are appropriate on the beach, but they should be covered up in public places like restaurants and stores.

- Resort casual clothing, such as shirts, shorts, and casual dresses, is the norm in dining establishments and resorts. Unless the venue specifies otherwise, formal attire is not required.

Etiquette for Photography

- Before shooting pictures of residents, especially in more remote places, always get their permission.

- Respect private property and places of cultural significance by not snapping photos where it is prohibited.

Environmental Respect

- The Virgin Islands National Park is a protected area located on St. John. Observe all park regulations, such as following trails, refraining from plant picking, and showing consideration for wildlife.

- Always take out everything you bring in, including rubbish, and refrain from littering or upsetting natural habitats.

- By adhering to these safety precautions and etiquette rules, you will contribute to maintaining St. John's integrity and making travel enjoyable and courteous for both tourists and residents.

Bonus

Importance of the Bonus: Simple Common Phrases to Help You Interact Like a Local

This bonus section is an essential part of the St. John Travel Guide, as it helps visitors connect with the local community in a meaningful way. Using simple, local phrases shows respect for the culture and enhances the travel experience. It helps foster positive interactions, creates goodwill with residents, and allows you to better navigate everyday situations, from ordering food to asking for directions. Mastering a few local phrases not only makes your trip more immersive but also makes you feel more at home on the island. Whether you're shopping at a market or chatting with locals, speaking their language, even just a little, can go a long way in building rapport and showing appreciation for their way of life.

Common and Useful Phrases to Interact with Locals in St. John

- Good Morning / Good Afternoon / Good Evening
    - "Good morning!" – *"Bonjou!"*
    - "Good afternoon!" – *"Bon aprèmidi!"*
    - "Good evening!" – *"Bon swa!"*
- How are you?
    - *"Kijan ou ye?"* (Informal)
    - *"Kijan ou ye, manman?"* (More formal, addressing an elder or respectfully)
- I'm fine, thank you.
    - *"Mwen byen, mèsi."*
- Please
    - *"Tanpri."*
- Thank you
    - *"Mèsi."*
- You're welcome
    - *"Pa gen pwoblem."*
- Excuse me
    - *"Eskize mwen."*
- How much does this cost?
    - *"Konbyen sa koute?"*
- Where is...?
    - *"Kote ...?"*
      (Example: "Where is the beach?" – *"Kote plaj la?"*)
- I don't understand.
    - *"Mwen pa konprann."*
- Do you speak English?
    - *"Eske ou pale Anglè?"*
- Yes / No
    - *"Wi" / "Non"*
- What time is it?
    - *"Ki lè li ye?"*
- I would like...
    - *"Mwen ta renmen..."*
- Can you help me?
    - *"Eske ou ka ede mwen?"*

83

- Where can I find...?

    - *"Kote mwen ka jwenn ...?"*
       (Example: "Where can I find food?" – *"Kote mwen ka jwenn manje?"*)
- I am lost.

    - *"Mwen pèdi."*
- Is this the way to...?

    - *"Èske sa se chemen pou ...?"*
       (Example: "Is this the way to the ferry?" – *"Èske sa se chemen pou ferry a?"*)
- I need a taxi.

    - *"Mwen bezwen yon taksi."*
- I am looking for...

    - *"Mwen ap chèche ..."*
       (Example: "I am looking for a place to eat." – *"Mwen ap chèche yon kote pou manje."*)
- What's your name?

    - *"Kijan ou rele?"*
- My name is...

    - *"Non mwen se..."*
- Goodbye

    - *"Orevwa!"*
       or *"A la pwochen!"* (See you later)

These phrases will help you interact more easily and respectfully with the locals, enhancing your travel experience in St. John.

TRAVEL JOURNAL

Date	Destination/Stop	Key Activities/Excursions	Memorable Moments	Food Tried/Restaurants	Thoughts & Reflections	Photos Taken (Yes/No)
Day 1						
Day 2						
Day 3						
Day 4						
Day 5						
Day 6						
Day 7						
Packing List:		Special Memories to Remember:			Important Contacts/Information	

Contact details and helpful websites for visitors

Overview and Resources for Visitors

Visitusvi.com is the website of the U.S. Virgin Islands Department of Tourism.

Offers basic information on lodging, activities, and attractions in St. John and the entire U.S. Virgin Islands. Phone: +1 800-372-8784; email: info@usvitourism.vi.

Website of the St. John Information Center: www.stjohnusvi.com

- **Telephone**: (340) 776-6344
- provides useful information on St. John, such as a guide to beaches, hiking trails, restaurants, and activities, along with local insights.

Moving around

- Website for the Virgin Islands Ferry Service: www.vi-ferry.com
- Telephone: (340) 776-6296
- Information about ferry timetables and pricing for trips between St. John, St. Thomas, and other neighboring islands is provided.

Phone number for the St. John Taxi Association: +1 340-774-3137

- URL: www.sjta.org.

Offers taxi services, along with information on how to navigate around St. John, rates, and reservations.

- Website for St. John Rental Cars: www.stjohnrentacar.com
- Telephone: (340) 776-2440

allows you to rent a car and explore the island at your speed.

Accommodations

- Website for Caneel Bay Resort: www.caneelbay.com
- Telephone: (340) 776-611
- Beautiful beachfront lodging is available at this opulent resort in Virgin Islands National Park.

The website for the Westin St. John Resort Villas is www.marriott.com.

- **Telephone**: (340) 776-0001
- A large resort on the island's stunning north shore featuring villas and a variety of dining options.

Website for Gallows Point Resort: www.gallowspoint.com

- **Telephone**: (340) 693-8333
- A boutique hotel close to Cruz Bay that offers charming views and a cozy stay.

Tours & Activities

- **Phone**: +1 340-776-6201; Website: www.nps.gov/viis; Virgin Islands National Park
- provides details about visitor centers, park trails, and conservation initiatives.

Website for Eco Tours St. John: www.ecotoursstjohn.com

- **Telephone**: (340) 779-2155
- offers environmentally friendly St. John trips that include hiking, snorkeling, and sightseeing activities.

Surf and Dive Adventures in the Virgin Islands: www.virginislandssnorkelanddiveadventures.com

Telephone: (340) 693-3474

- specializes in customized diving and snorkeling excursions around the top locations in St. John.

Emergency Assistance

- Phone: +1 340-776-6400 Myrah Keating Smith Community Health Center
- The primary medical center in St. John provides emergency care and medical services.

Phone number for the St. John Police Department: +1 340-776-1123

- For reporting crimes, police emergencies, and safety issues.

Forecast and Weather

- St. Thomas Office of the U.S. National Weather Service Phone: +1 340-776-8500 Website: www.weather.gov/tlh
- gives the most recent weather predictions and reports for the Virgin Islands and St. John.

These tools, which include everything from transportation to emergency contact information, can assist in guaranteeing a seamless and knowledgeable trip to St. John.

Greetings, Traveler

First and foremost, I would like to sincerely thank you for selecting St. John Travel Guide: A Comprehensive Guide to Authentic Local Experiences, Hiking Trails, and Pristine Beaches. I put my heart and soul into it, in addition to my time and effort, because it has been a labor of love.

As you may be aware, writing a guidebook involves more than just gathering facts; it also entails encapsulating a location, establishing a connection with its soul, and showcasing its splendor to future generations. The trip to St. John was no easy task. To make sure you get the most accurate, useful, and perceptive information for your trip, it requires many hours of research, travel, and first-hand experiences.

St. John's immaculate beaches, stunning trails, and lively culture have made a lasting impression. I sincerely hope that my guide helped you experience the island's beauty. Everything was planned with you in mind, from the greatest places to snorkel to the best secret restaurants, so you could enjoy St. John in all its splendor.

I would be extremely appreciative if you could take a moment to provide a good review if you found this guide useful and if it assisted you in organizing an unforgettable trip. Your criticism is a major factor in my development as a travel guide author, not just a reflection of the work completed. Good reviews encourage me to keep writing in-depth guides that assist tourists like you to get the most out of their trips and help me hone my skills.

Furthermore, the purpose of all the time, money, and effort that went into this project was to give you the greatest experience possible. In addition to supporting this work, your review will help other travelers make wise choices and have a great time when visiting St. John. Your encouraging remarks are what fuel my enthusiasm and forward my goal of offering worthwhile, dependable, and remarkable travel information.

Again, I want to thank you for entrusting your St. John adventure to this guide. I hope you were able to discover the island's hidden gems, take in its breathtaking scenery, and make lifelong memories.

With sincere gratitude and admiration.